JINN & BLACK MAGIC

Dr. Ali's Pearls of Lectures Series

JINN & BLACK MAGIC

*Understanding
The Reality & Seeking Remedies
in Islamic Theology.*

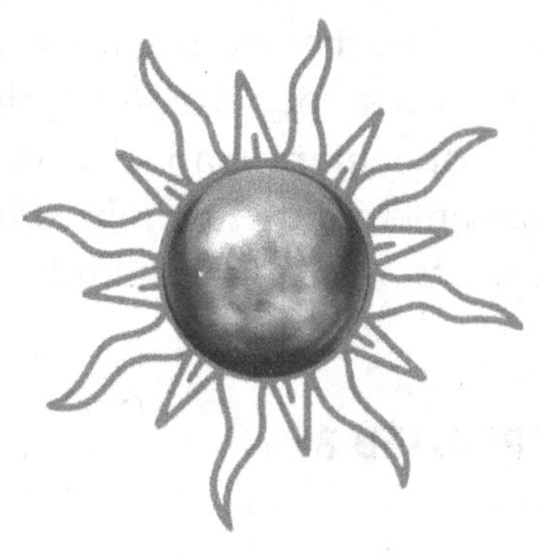

DR. ALI MOHAMED SALAH.

1445/2024

LOOH PRESS LTD.
Copyright © Ali Mohamed Salah 2024
First Edition, First Print June 2024

PRINTED & DISTRIBUTED BY
Looh Press Ltd.
56 Lethbridge Close
Leicester, England. UK
www.LoohPress.com
LoohPress@gmail.com

CONTACT AUTHOR
Ali.Kuantan@gmail.com

A catalogue record of this title is available from the British Library.

Edited and Cover Design   : Looh Press
Typeset   : Kusmin (Looh Press)

ISBN: 978-82-693677-4-4   (Paperback Cover)

TRANSLITERATION TABLE

(ء) = '	(ا) = a / A / ā / Ā	(ب) = b / B
(ت) = t / T	(ث) = th / TH	(ج) = j / J
(ح) = ḥ / Ḥ	(خ) = kh / KH	(د) = d / D
(ذ) = dh / DH	(ر) = r / R	(ز) = z / Z
(س) = s / S	(ش) = sh / SH	(ص) = ṣ / Ṣ
(ض) = ḍ / Ḍ	(ط) = ṭ / Ṭ	(ظ) = ẓ / Ẓ
(ع) = ' / '	(غ) = gh / GH	(ف) = f / F
(ق) = q / Q	(ك) = k / K	(ل) = l / L
(م) = m / M	(ن) = n / N	(ه) = h / H
(و) = w / W / ū / Ū	(ي) = y / Y / ī /	

ﷻ	=	Jalla Jallāluhu
﷽	=	Subḥānahu Wa Taʿālā
؏	=	ʿAlayhis-Salām
ﷺ	=	Sallalāhu ʿAlayhi Wasallam
﵀	=	Raḥimahu Allāh
؆	=	Raḍiyallāhu ʿanhu
؇	=	Raḍiyallāhu ʿanhā
؈	=	Raḍiyallāhu ʿanhumā

الله	=	Allah
سبحانه و تعالى	=	Subhanahu wa-ta'ala
ﷺ	=	Sallalahu Alayhi Wasalam
التوحيد	=	Tawheed
رحمه الله	=	Rahimahu Allah
السنة	=	SUNNAH
رضي الله عنه	=	Radi Allahu anhu
رضى الله عنهما	=	Radi Allahu Anhuma
رضى الله عنها	=	Raḍi Allah anhā
الرحمن	=	al-Rahman
شريعة	=	Sharia
اخلاق	=	Akhlaq
عقيدة	=	Aqedah
عبادة	=	Ibadah
معاملة	=	mu'amalat
معروف	=	Ma'ruf
تصوّف	=	al-tasawwuf
آيات	=	Ayat
طاعة	=	da'ah
بدعة	=	BID'AH
بدعة حسن	=	bid'ah hasanah
الخلفاء الراشدون	=	al-khulafa' al-raashidoon
ردة	=	riddah
كفر	=	kufr
التقو	=	Taqwa
صَوْم	=	Sawm
عدة	=	Iddah
فتنة	=	Fitnah
التربية	=	Tarbiyah
اعتكاف	=	i'tikaf
حلال	=	Halal
حرام	=	Haram

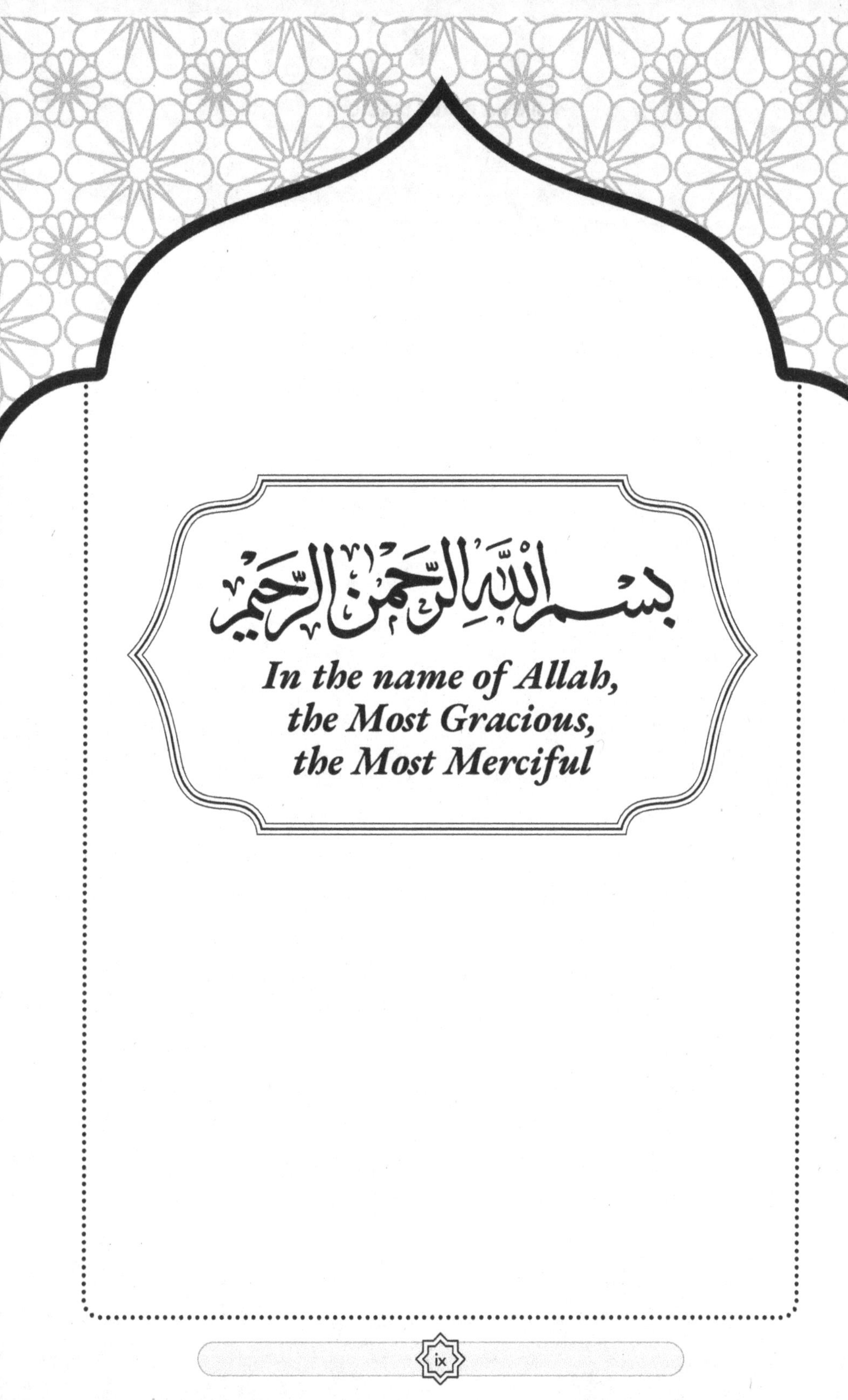

In the name of Allah,
the Most Gracious,
the Most Merciful

DEDICATION

I dedicate this humble writing to the souls of my beloved parents, who steadfastly supported me throughout my long educational journey. I also dedicate it to my family, whose patience and understanding during my writing and devotion to Dawah activities have been invaluable. They have generously sacrificed their time for me. May Allah ﷻ reward them with the best in this world and the hereafter.

ACKNOWLEDGMENT

I hereby express my profound gratitude to everyone who has generously contributed to the writing of this book in any capacity. Among those I wholeheartedly thank is Mohammed Isak Abdullahi, whose efforts were instrumental in the creation of this work. He voluntarily collected and transcribed several of my English lectures from various YouTube channels and provided them to me. This was the most invaluable gift I could receive, as it saved me considerable time and energy in gathering new material. In addition to this, Mohammed Isak Abdullahi also offered technical support, enabling the book to be produced in its current form. I pray that Allah rewards him abundantly in this world and the hereafter for his contributions.

LIST OF TERMS

TERM	BRIEF DESCRIPTION
ʿIFRĪT	Type of Jinn with exceptional strength, intelligence, and invulnerability occupying a prominent and formidable position within their ranks.
HĀRŪT & MĀRŪT	Harut and Marut are the two angels, mentioned in the Quran. They were sent by Allah to the city of Babylon to test the faith of its inhabitants.
IBLĪS	is a being created from fire and is from the jinn. Initially, Allah granted him a rank similar to that of the angels. However, when he disobeyed Allah, he was cursed due to his rebelliousness and disobedience.
JINN JĀNN	JINN (singular: jinni; also spelled djinni or genie) is an Arabic word meaning "to hide." Jinn are supernatural beings in Islamic and Arabic texts, created from "smokeless and scorching fire," distinct from humans and angels.. JĀNN:serpent-like, primitive, and considered the father of the jinn

KARĀMĀT	(singular: karāmah) refers to miraculous deeds or supernatural events attributed to Muslim saints (awliya) or pious individuals in Islamic tradition. These miracles are considered signs of divine favor and are believed to occur through the power and will of Allah ﷻ, rather than the individual's own abilities
QARĪN	is a type of jinn believed to accompany every human being from birth. The term "qarīn" means "constant companion" or "associate." This being is often understood to have a negative influence, whispering evil thoughts and temptations to lead a person astray.
RUQYAH	Ruqyah is the practice of using incantations, prayers, and verses from the Quran for healing and protection against various ailments, including physical, mental, and spiritual issues. It is a form of Islamic spiritual healing and exorcism, often used to ward off evil spirits (jinn), the evil eye, and black magic.
RĀQĪ	is an individual who performs ruqyah, the practice of reciting Quranic verses and prayers for healing and protection.
SHAYṬĀN	the evil jinn, akin to demons in Christianity. In Islam, these jinn chose to be non-Muslim.

SIḤR	also spelled as "sorcery" or "black magic," is the practice of using supernatural forces, often with evil intent, to manipulate or control events, people, or circumstances.
SIḤR AL-TAFRĪQ	refers to a specific type of sorcery or black magic in Islamic tradition that aims to create discord, division, or separation between people, especially within families or between spouses
ṢIḤR AT-TIWALAH	Siḥr al-Tiwala or Siḥr al-Maḥaba, which can be translated as "magic of love" or "magic of infatuation," involves seeking to gain the affection of a spouse through magical means.
ṢIḤR AL_KHAYAL AT-TAKHYĪL	Siḥr al-Khayāl, also known as "illusionary sorcery" or "magic of the imagination," is a type of black magic practiced with the intention of creating illusions or hallucinations in the mind of the victim. This form of sorcery aims to deceive and manipulate the senses, leading the targeted individual to perceive things that are not real or to experience distorted perceptions of reality.
SIḤR AL-UQM	Siḥr of al-Uqm is a form of black magic aimed at causing sterility, thereby preventing a woman from conceiving.

ṢIḤR AL-JUNŪN	Ṣiḥr al-Junūn, also known as "magic of madness," is a type of sorcery practiced with the intention of inducing mental illness or insanity in the victim. This form of black magic aims to destabilize the mental faculties and psychological well-being of the targeted individual, leading to symptoms of madness or irrational behavior
ṢIḤR AL-KHUMŪL	Ṣiḥr al-Khumūl, also known as "magic of drowsiness," is a type of sorcery practiced with the intent to induce excessive sleepiness or drowsiness in the victim. This form of black magic aims to disrupt the victim's wakefulness and alertness, leading to lethargy, fatigue, and a general state of drowsiness.
ṢIḤR AL-HAWĀTIF	Ṣiḥr al-Hawātif, also known as "magic of whisperings," is a form of sorcery aimed at manipulating or controlling a person's thoughts or inner perceptions. This type of black magic targets the inner faculties of the mind, influencing the victim's thoughts, beliefs, and perceptions through whisperings or suggestion
ṢIḤR AL-MARAD	Ṣiḥr al-Marad, also known as "magic of sickness," is a form of sorcery aimed at causing physical illness or ailment in the victim. This type of black magic targets the body, leading to the manifestation of various sicknesses, diseases, or ailments

ṢIḤR AN-NAZIF	Ṣiḥr an-Nazīf refers to a type of sorcery that may result in continuous bleeding outside of the normal menstrual cycle for women.
WASWASA	refers to whispers or intrusive thoughts that arise in the mind, particularly those of a negative or doubtful nature. In Islamic context, waswasa often refers to the whisperings of Shayṭān (Satan) aimed at causing doubt, anxiety, or confusion in a person's faith or actions.

CONTENTS

ABSTRACT

This book aims to unveil the nature of Satan as described in the Quran and prophetic tradition, while also offering insights from Christian and Judeo-Biblical studies. It delves into the complex nature of the devil as an entity and explores its influence on humanity. Thoroughly examining Satan's tactics and schemes to mislead humanity, the book provides guidance on how to struggle against its deception and ultimately overcome it.

In addition, the book explores the reality of black magic, its implications, and potential remedies. It highlights the unequivocal condemnation of black magic in Islam, deeming it one of the gravest sins. Islam staunchly denounces black magic due to its impurity and deviation from the divine path of truth and purity ordained by Allah ﷻ. Engaging in black magic only leads to further harm and spiritual degradation, diverting believers from goodness and blessings.

Through this comprehensive analysis, the book seeks to offer a deeper understanding of both the nature of the devil and the severe consequences of engaging in black magic, providing readers with the knowledge and tools to safeguard their spiritual well-being.

INTRODUCTION

Indeed, all praise and thanks are due to Allah ﷻ. We praise Him, we seek His assistance, we seek His forgiveness, and we seek His guidance. Whomsoever Allah misguides, no one can guide, and whom Allah guides, no one can misguide, and I bear witness that there is no one worthy of worship save Allah, and Muhammad ﷺ is his final Messenger.

While writing "Exploring the Evil Eye: Reality and Remedy - An Islamic Perspective," I considered including chapters on the Jinn and black magic. These three topics form an interconnected triangle, sharing similar symptoms and treatments, with Ruqya serving as the primary method of treatment and protection. However, to avoid overwhelming the reader, I decided to focus exclusively on the evil eye in that book and to address Jinn and black magic in a separate volume.

As I was gathering data for my new project on Jinn and black magic, I considered the idea of collecting some of my English lectures from YouTube using Vizard.ai. Among the collected lectures were "Devil's Deception," delivered at Oslo University on October 23, 2010, and "Black Magic: Cures and Protection," presented at the Peace Conference Scandinavia organized by IslamNet on March 21, 2016. This method of collecting lectures significantly reduced the effort required to gather data for my new book on Jinn and black magic.

Given that these lectures were delivered orally, they required

thorough rectification, refinement, and revision to ensure linguistic accuracy. Additionally, it was necessary to authenticate and footnote the information from original sources to make the content suitable for academic reading. The process of arranging and refining the book took considerable time, nearly equivalent to writing a new book from scratch.

The topics covered in this book are of paramount importance as they address numerous questions about the realm of hidden spirits. The significance of this work is underscored by the current era, where truth and falsehood often intermingle, and the pursuit of knowledge is frequently neglected.

This book is part of a series of writings aimed at raising awareness, particularly among the younger English-speaking generation, who are eager to learn about Islam's perspectives on complex theological issues. To meet these needs, I present this book titled "Jinn and Black Magic: Understanding the Reality and Seeking Remedies in Islamic Theology."

I hope, Inshallah, that this book, along with other distinguished works on the topic by esteemed authors in various languages, will clarify ambiguities and provide answers to frequently asked questions.

Dr. Ali Mohamed Salah
Dhul Qa'dah 1445 / May 2024

CHAPTER 01

DEVIL'S DECEPTION

SECTION ONE
HIDDEN SPIRITS: AN EXAMINATION OF THEIR DEFINITION AND CREATION

DELIVERED	23rd of January 2010 Oslo University (organized by IslamNet)

THE MEANING AND SIGNIFICANCE OF JINN, JĀNN, SATAN, DEVIL, IBLĪS, ʿIFRĪT, AND QARĪN WITHIN THE CONTEXT OF ISLAMIC THEOLOGY

Before embarking on distinguishing these terms, it's imperative to cite a Quranic verse where each is referenced, along with the frequency of their mention in the Quran:

1- The term **"al-Jānn"** is mentioned in the Holy Quran 7 times. One instance is as follows:

"And the (al-jānn) Jinn race, We had Created before, from the fire Of a scorching wind".[1]

2- The term **"al-Jinn"** 22 times. One instance is as follows:

"I have only created Jinns and men, that They may serve Me."[2]

3- **Satan**, 75 times. One instance is as follows:

"Verily Satan is an enemy To you : so treat him As an enemy. He only Invites his adherents, That they may become Companions of the Blazing Fire"[3]

4- **Iblīs** was mentioned in the Quran **11 times**, One instance is as follows:

"(God) said : " O Iblīs ! what prevents thee from Prostrating thyself to one Whom I have created With My hands ? Art thou haughty ? Or art thou one Of the high (and mighty) ones ?"[4]

5- **'Ifrīt** was mentioned only **once** in a single Sūra:

"Said an 'Ifrīt, of the Jinns"[5]

6- **Qarīn**: The mention of **"Jinn Companionship"** is limited

---

1 Sūra 15: Hijr, 27

2 Sūra 51: Zāriyāt, 56

3 Sūra 35: Fātir, 6

4 Sūra 38: Sād, 75

5 Sūra 27: Naml, 39

to just four instances where it explicitly refers to jinn. However, there are other occurrences where "Qarīn" is mentioned without specifically referring to jinn. One of the four instances is as follows:

"And We have destined For them intimate companions (Of like nature), who made Alluring to them what was Before them and behind them ; And the sentence among The previous generations of Jinns And men, who have passed away, Is proved against them ; For they are utterly lost".[6]

In Islamic theology, the concept of Jinn holds a significant place, mentioned twenty two times in the Qur'an and even dedicated a whole sura, "al-Jinn," which provides explicit insight into their nature. Described as a part of divine creation separate from humans and angels, yet sharing certain traits like intellect and freedom, Jinn are believed to inhabit a realm beyond human perception. Quranic verses such as sura al-Hijr verse 27 indicate their creation before mankind from smokeless fire, with exegetes suggesting that Jānn was the progenitor of the jinn, similar to Adam's role for humanity.

The jinn's existence is further elaborated upon in Islamic scholarship, noting their ability to eat, drink, and procreate, akin to humans. Some Jinn are depicted as righteous, while others are not, mirroring the diversity of human character. Notable exegetes like al-Ṭabarī emphasize the obligation of both humans and Jinn to worship and surrender to God.

Another pivotal figure in Islamic lore is Iblis, commonly known as the devil. Linguistically, the term ***"Iblīs"*** is believed

---

6 Sūra 41:Fussilat, 25

to stem from words denoting desperation or lack of benefit, indicating his defiance and despair of Allah's mercy. As the head of the Satan, Iblīs plays a central role in tempting mankind towards wickedness and disobedience.

The term **"Satan,"** or "Shayṭān," is derived from roots meaning "stay away" or "disrupt." It appears frequently in the Qur'an, with interpretations suggesting its association with entities that lead astray from truth. Additionally, the Qur'an introduces the concept of "al-Tāghūt," often equated with Satan in human form, emphasizing the pervasive influence of evil.[7]

It is commonly asserted by scholars that Jānn was the progenitor of the jinn, analogous to Adam's role as the father of mankind. This belief reflects the idea of lineage and origin within the Islamic cosmological framework, highlighting the parallel creation narratives for humans and jinn.

Moreover, in Tafsīr al-Miṣbāḥ, the term **"Ifrīt"** is interpreted as referring to a specific category of Jinn characterized by exceptional strength, intelligence, and invulnerability. This designation suggests a hierarchical classification among the jinn, with 'Ifrīt occupying a prominent and formidable position within their ranks.

The Qarīn accompanies every human, tempting them towards disobedience to Allah, except for the Prophet Muḥammad ﷺ. 'Abdallah b. Mas'ūd narrates the Prophet's acknowledgment of his own Jinn companion, subdued by Allah's intervention.

---

7   The Jinn, Devil and Satan: A Review on Qur'anic Concept September 2015Mediterranean Journal of Social Sciences 6(5) DOI:10.5901/mjss.2015.v6n5s1p540 LicenseCC BY-NC, https://www.researchgate.net/publication/282424716_The_Jinn_Devil_and_Satan_A_Review_on_Qur'anic_Concept

'Abdallah b. Mas'ūd reported that Allah's Messenger (ﷺ) said:

"There is none amongst you with whom is not an attache from amongst the Jinn (devil). They (the Companions) said: Allah's Messenger, with you too? Thereupon he said: Yes, but Allah helps me against him and so I am safe from his hand and he does not command me but for good".[8]

The Hadith reveals the Prophet's unique guidance towards righteousness, despite the innate tendency of Jinn companions to incite evil. Another report introduces the concept of dual companionship, including both Jinn and angels.

Allah ﷻ says:

"His Companion will say : " Our Lord ! I did not Make him transgress, But he was (himself) Far astray. "

He will say : " Dispute not With each other In My Presence : I had already in advance Sent you Warning.

" The Word changes not Before Me, and I do not The least injustice To My Servants"[9]

Ibn Kathīr's commentary on this verse elucidates the Qarīn's disavowal of its human companion on the Day of Judgment, denying responsibility for their transgressions.

The phrase *"Dispute not With each other In My Presence"* refers to what Allah ﷻ will say to the human and his companion

---

8   Sahih Muslim 2814a: Book 52, Hadith 62

9   Sūra 50: Qāf, 27-29

from among the jinn, when they dispute before Him., and the human says, 'O Lord, this one led me astray from the Reminder after it had come to me' and the devil will say, 'Our Lord! I did not push him to transgression, (in disbelief, oppression, and evil deeds), but he was himself in error far astray' – i.e., from the path of truth.

'Abdallah b. 'Umar reported that the Messenger of Allah ﷺ of Allah said:

"If anyone of you is praying, he should not let anyone pass in front of him; if that person insists then he should fight him for there is a Qarīn with him"[10]

The term '*Qarīn*' as explained in Al-Qamus, an Arabic-language dictionary, denotes a companion. It signifies that Shayṭān consistently accompanies and never forsakes mankind. This interpretation by Imam al-Shawkānī, clarifies the presence of the Qarīn, depicting a perpetual association with evil.[11]

This Qarīn remains with a person from birth until death, influencing their thoughts and actions. While angels encourage righteousness and good deeds, the qareen may tempt individuals to engage in sinful behavior.

In conclusion, Devil, or Satan, are one of the jinn, but the Qur'an also potrays them as rebellious angels, a belief that had arisen in Judaism and Christianity previously. The scholars agree the devil are the first creatures who refused to obey Allah's command to salute Adam[12]

---

10 Muslim, 506

11 Nayl al-Awtar, 3/7

12 ibid

UNDERSTANDING THE PURPOSE OF THE CREATION OF JINN AND MANKIND IN ISLAMIC THEOLOGY

Initially, it's crucial to underscore the linguistic intricacies inherent in Arabic terminology before delving further into the exploration of the purpose of creation. The term "jinn" carries the connotation of "hidden" or "concealed," implying their unseen existence. This linguistic subtlety offers a profound insight into the spiritual dimension occupied by the Jinn and their significance within Islamic cosmology.

Various terms such as devil, Satan, jinn, and Iblīs are employed in religious discourse to describe entities associated with malevolence or spiritual deception. However, it is imperative to recognize that these terms collectively refer to the same entity, namely the jinn.

In Arabic, "jinn" refers to anything concealed or hidden from sight, whether by the naked eye or advanced technology. They are entities unseen to humans, but they can observe us from places imperceptible to us, as mentioned in Allah's words:

Allah ﷻ says:

"O ye children of Adam! let not satan seduce you in the same manner as he got your parents out of the garden stripping them of their raiment to expose their shame: for he and his tribe watch you from a position where ye cannot see them: We made the evil ones friends (only) to those without faith."[13]

---

13 Sūra 7: A'rāf, 27

This means that while they observe us, we remain unaware of their presence. Allah ﷻ emphasizes that these unseen entities possess the ability to perceive us, even when we are unable to perceive them. This aspect of divine revelation indicates the necessity of belief. Furthermore, this Quranic verse suggests the existence of a realm where our conventional understanding of physics does not hold true.

Islamic contemporary experts generally acknowledge the existence of Jinn as described in the Qur'an. There are three main opinions regarding the nature of jinn:

i) Some believe that Jinn have potentially negative influences, often tempting people towards evil. They may not have physical forms outside of humans but exist in a realm beyond human perception. This view is supported by verses like Sura al-Shams (The Sun) verse 8 and Sura al-Hijr (The Rocky Tract) verse 27, which indicate the creation of Jinn before Adam.

ii) Others see Jinn as akin to germs or viruses, lacking rationality and not obligated to embrace Islam. Scholars like Muḥammad 'Abdūh and Rashīd Riḍā hold this view, though 'Abdūh doesn't entirely deny the existence of Jinn in his Qur'anic exegesis.

iii) Another perspective regards Jinn as wild creatures inhabiting remote areas such as jungles and mountains, without civilization. This opinion was articulated by Aḥmad Khan.[14]

The purpose behind the creation of Jinn and humanity in Islamic theology is commonly understood as centered on the worship of Allah ﷻ, yet scholars have delved into various interpretations to explore additional underlying reasons and benefits.

---

14 The Jinn, Devil and Satan: A Review on Qur'anic Concept

Some assert that this purpose of worship is exclusively attributed to believers, implying that only faithful Jinn and humans are created for this specific task. This perspective, advocated by Daḥḥāk, Sufyān Thawrī, and others, emphasizes the steadfast commitment of believers to worship. A variant interpretation, ascribed to Ibn ʿAbbās, includes the term "believers" in the verse, reinforcing the notion that the directive pertains solely to them.[15]

Another explanation posits that while Allah ﷻ has enjoined worship upon all, individuals possess free will, enabling them to choose between righteous worship and deviation. This aligns with Sayyidna ʿAlī's assertion, as cited by al-Nasafī[16], which suggests that every Jinn and human possesses an inherent capacity for worship. Some utilize this capacity appropriately and attain success, while others misuse it by succumbing to sin and base desires, thereby corrupting it. In the Quran, Allah ﷻ states:

"I have only created Jinns and men, that They may serve Me."[17]

This verse indicates a profound purpose behind the creation of both Jinn and mankind: to worship Allah ﷻ. This verse is regarded as one of the most explicit elucidations in the Quran concerning the raison d'être of these two creations. It emphasizes that their fundamental purpose lies in devotion to Allah ﷻ.

"O ye assembly of Jinns and men! came there not unto

---

15 Tafsīr al-Nasafi, 1705/3, Imam Abdullah bin Ahmed bin Muhammad al+Nasafi, Darul Qalam, Beirut, 1st edition 1989

16 ibid

17 Sūra 51: Zāriyāt, 56

you apostles from amongst you setting forth unto you of the meeting of this day of yours?"[18]

"Many are the Jinns and men We have made for Hell: They have hearts wherewith they understand not eyes wherewith they see not and ears wherewith they hear not. They are like cattle nay more misguided: for they are heedless (of warning)."[19]

These verses elucidate the purpose of creation for both Jinn and humans, highlighting their accountability for their actions. They underscore that individuals from both entities will be either rewarded for their virtuous deeds or punished for their transgressions.

This interpretation underscores a fundamental principle within Islamic theology, elucidating the intrinsic connection between creation and devotion to the divine. The verse is a cornerstone for understanding the spiritual purpose behind the existence of sentient beings in Islamic thought.

Scholars, such as al-Ṭabarī[20] and al-Rāzī[21], interpret Quranic verses to assert that Jinn are bound by Islamic law just like humans, obligated to follow divine commands and avoid prohibitions. The Jinn are portrayed as beings with intellect and free will, capable of choosing between right and wrong. Some among them have embraced the teachings of Prophet Muḥammad, indicating their inclusion in divine creation and their capacity for righteousness.[22]

---

18 Sūra 6: An'ām, 130

19 Sūra 7: A'rāf, 179

20 https://shamela.ws/book/7798/14612

21 https://tafsir.app/alrazi/51/55

22 The Jinn, Devil and Satan: A Review on Qur'anic Concept

SECTION TWO
CONFRONTING THE ADVERSARY: STRATEGIES AGAINST SPIRITUAL DECEPTION IN ABRAHAMIC FAITH TRADITIONS

WARNINGS AGAINST SATAN IN THE BIBLE

The inquiry into how to confront the deceptive tactics of the devil is a significant aspect of spiritual discourse across Abrahamic faith traditions. It is acknowledged that the devil operates through various forms of deception, seeking to lead individuals away from the path of righteousness.

Understanding how to effectively counter these attacks

requires a comprehensive exploration of religious teachings and spiritual practices.

It is essential to recognize the devil as a distinct entity within religious cosmologies. Across Abrahamic faiths, including Judaism, Christianity, and Islam, the devil is depicted as a malevolent being who opposes the divine will. In Islamic theology, the devil, known as Shayṭān or Iblīs, is considered a created being, much like humans, with the capacity for intellect and agency. This understanding aligns with the broader theological framework of monotheism, wherein God is the ultimate creator and sustainer of all beings, including the devil.

Furthermore, examining the portrayal of the devil within Judeo-Christian traditions provides valuable insights into the nature of spiritual deception. In these traditions, the devil is often depicted as a cunning adversary who tempts individuals to disobey God's commandments. Through careful study of religious texts such as the Bible and Talmud, one can glean wisdom regarding the strategies employed by the devil and how righteous individuals resisted his influence.

In the Bible, particularly in the New Testament, the devil is depicted as a real entity with malevolent intentions towards humanity. Numerous passages warn believers about the adversary, urging them to remain vigilant against his schemes. One notable example is found in 1 Peter 5:8, which states,

"Be alert and of sober mind. Your enemy the devil prowls around like a roaring lion looking for someone to devour."[23]

---

23 1 Peter 5:8, https://www.biblegateway.com/passage/?search=1%20Peter%20
5%3A8&version=NIV

This imagery vividly portrays the active threat posed by the devil, likening him to a predatory beast seeking to destroy those who stray from the path of righteousness.

Similarly, throughout the Bible, the devil is described using symbolic language that underscores his role as the embodiment of darkness and temptation. Terms such as "Prince of Darkness" or "Kng of the Darkness" evoke the pervasive influence of evil in the world and the constant struggle between light and darkness. These descriptive phrases serve to emphasize the power and malevolence attributed to the devil within biblical narratives.

Furthermore, biblical characters often encounter the devil in various forms, engaging in spiritual battles against his deceptive tactics.

The story of Jesus' temptation in the wilderness, as recounted in the Gospels of Matthew, Mark, and Luke, illustrates this conflict, with the devil tempting Jesus with worldly desires in an attempt to derail his divine mission. This narrative is a paradigmatic example of the spiritual warfare depicted throughout the Bible, highlighting the ongoing struggle between good and evil.

The biblical portrayal of the devil aligns closely with the perspective presented in the Quran, emphasizing the reality of the devil as a genuine adversary intent on leading humanity astray.

In the Bible, particularly in the New Testament, there are various references to Satan as a formidable adversary who seeks to undermine humanity's relationship with God. One such analogy is found in 1 Peter 5:8, which likens Satan to a roaring lion seeking to devour his prey.

"Be self-controlled and alert. Your enemy the devil

prowls around like a roaring lion looking for someone to devour. 9Resist him, standing firm in the faith, because you know that your brothers throughout the world are undergoing the same kind of sufferings".[24]

This imagery emphasizes the relentless and predatory nature of evil, suggesting that Satan is relentless in his efforts to lead people astray.

Furthermore, the Bible attributes the introduction of sin into the world to the actions of Satan. The story of Adam and Eve in Genesis portrays Satan, in the form of a serpent, tempting them to disobey God's command, thus ushering sin into the world. This narrative underscores Satan's role as a deceiver and instigator of disobedience.

Additionally, the Bible associates various forms of suffering and spiritual alienation with the influence of Satan. For instance, in the Book of Job, Satan is depicted as the instigator of suffering and hardship in Job's life, testing his faithfulness to God. This reflects the belief that Satan is not only responsible for introducing sin but also for perpetuating spiritual discord and adversity in the world.

Moreover, the Bible portrays Satan as a tempter, using various tactics to lead individuals away from the path of righteousness. This aligns with the Quranic depiction of Iblīs as a deceiver who seeks to misguide humanity. Both traditions emphasize the need for vigilance and spiritual resilience in resisting temptation and remaining steadfast in faith.

"Now the serpent was more cunning than any beast of the

---

24 1 Peter 5:8, https://goodnewsuk.com/bible-helps/1-peter-58-10

field which the LORD God had made. And he said to the woman, "Has God indeed said, "You shall not eat of every tree of the garden"?" And the woman said to the serpent, "We may eat the fruit of the trees of the garden; but of the fruit of the tree which is in the midst of the garden, God has said, "You shall not eat it, nor shall you touch it, lest you die."" Then the serpent said to the woman, "You will not surely die. For God knows that in the day you eat of it your eyes will be opened, and you will be like God, knowing good and evil."[25]

"You are of your father the devil, and the desires of your father you want to do. He was a murderer from the beginning, and does not stand in the truth, because there is no truth in him. When he speaks a lie, he speaks from his own resources, for he is a liar and the father of it."[26]

"Put on the whole armor of God, that you may be able to stand against the wiles of the devil".[27]

"And the LORD God said to the woman, "What is this you have done?" The woman said, "The serpent deceived me, and I ate."[28]

"How you are fallen from heaven,
O Lucifer, son of the morning!

---

25 Genesis 3:1-5 https://www.cgg.org/index.cfm/library/verses/id/5334/satan-as-tempter-verses.htm

26 John 8:44 https://www.cgg.org/index.cfm/library/verses/id/5334/satan-as-tempter-verses.htm

27 Ephesians 6:11 https://www.cgg.org/index.cfm/library/verses/id/5334/satan-as-tempter-verses.htm

28 Genesis 3:13 https://www.cgg.org/index.cfm/library/verses/id/5334/satan-as-tempter-verses.htm

How you are cut down to the ground,
You who weakened the nations![29]

"And do not lead us into temptation,
But deliver us from the evil one.

For Yours is the kingdom and the power and the glory forever. Amen".[30]

"Now when the devil had ended every temptation, he departed from Him until an opportune time".[31]

Both Quranic and Biblical teachings acknowledge the concept of human free will and responsibility in resisting temptation and avoiding sin. While Satan may tempt and deceive, it is ultimately up to individuals to choose whether to succumb to these influences or to resist them. In the Bible, James 1:14-15 explains this concept, stating,

"but each person is tempted when they are dragged away by their own evil desire and enticed. 15 Then, after desire has conceived, it gives birth to sin; and sin, when it is full-grown, gives birth to death".[32]

This passage underscores the idea that sin originates from within individuals, arising from their own desires and choices.

---

29 Isaiah 14:12 https://www.cgg.org/index.cfm/library/verses/id/5334/satan-as-tempt-er-verses.htm

30 Matthew 6:13 https://www.cgg.org/index.cfm/library/verses/id/5334/sa-tan-as-tempter-verses.htm

31 Luke 4:13 https://www.cgg.org/index.cfm/library/verses/id/5334/satan-as-tempt-er-verses.htm

32 James 1:14-15, https://www.biblegateway.com/passage/?search=James%20 1%3A14-15&version=NIV

Furthermore, the Bible warns against giving the devil a foothold in one's life through continued disobedience and lawlessness. Ephesians 4:27 cautions,

"and do not give the devil a foothold." [33]

This admonition underscores the importance of personal responsibility in resisting temptation and maintaining spiritual integrity.

The characterization of evil entities in the Bible underscores their formidable nature, emphasizing traits such as cunning, intelligence, and a relentless propensity for leading individuals astray. These depictions caution against underestimating the malevolent forces that seek to disrupt moral and spiritual integrity.

Furthermore, a comparative analysis of religious scriptures and cultural heritages reveals common themes regarding the nature of evil and the devil. While Islam is often noted for its detailed discussions on these topics, it is imperative to recognize that similar portrayals exist in other religious traditions. The notion of a malevolent force antagonistic to divine order and human welfare transcends specific religious boundaries, manifesting in diverse mythologies and theological narratives.

This comparative approach extends beyond religious studies to encompass broader academic inquiries into the nature of evil and its manifestations in human culture and psychology. Scholars across various disciplines explore the complexities of morality, spirituality, and the human condition, acknowledging the pervasive influence of narratives surrounding the struggle between good and evil.

---

33 Ephesians 4:27 https://www.bibleref.com/Ephesians/4/Ephesians-4-27.html

GUARDING AGAINST THE SCHEMES OF SHAYṬĀN IN ISLAM: WARNINGS AND VIGILANCE

Before delving into the specifics of theological discourse concerning Jinn and spiritual struggle, it is imperative to acknowledge the broader context of Islamic eschatology and the cosmic battle between good and evil. Islamic theology acknowledges the existence of malevolent forces seeking to lead humanity astray and emphasizes the importance of spiritual vigilance and adherence to divine guidance in resisting temptation and deception.

Islam teaches that Satan, known as "Shayṭān" or "Iblīs," actively seeks to lead humans astray from the path of righteousness. Various methods of satanic influence are described, including whisperings (waswasa) and temptations aimed at undermining faith and morality. Believers are advised to remain vigilant and seek refuge in Allah ﷻ from the snares of Satan, adhering to moral principles and performing acts of worship to strengthen their spiritual defenses.

In Islam, understanding the struggle against Satan's deception is crucial. Allah ﷻ instructs us in the Quran that Satan is our enemy, and we should treat him as such. Allah ﷻ says:

"Verily Satan is an enemy To you : so treat him As an enemy. He only Invites his adherents, That they may become Companions of the Blazing Fire"[34]

Satan's invitation aims to lead people astray and ultimately to become dwellers of the blazing fire, destined for Hell. Allah ﷻ warns us not to join his party or fall into his category. His mission is clear: to gather followers for the inhabitants of Hellfire.

---

34 Sūra 35: Fātir, 6

Allah ﷻ states in the Holy Quran that Satan has been and continues to be a clear enemy to humanity. This enmity dates back to the expulsion of Adam and Eve from Paradise, an event orchestrated by Satan, also known as Iblīs, as mentioned in the following Quranic verses:

"We had already, beforehand, Taken the covenant of Adam, But he forgot : and We found On his part no firm resolve.

When We said to the angels, " Prostrate yourselves to Adam ", They prostrated themselves, but not Iblīs : he refused.

Then We said : " O Adam ! Verily, this is an enemy To thee and thy wife : So let him not get you Both out of the Garden, So that thou art landed In misery.

" There is therein (enough provision) For thee not to go hungry Nor to go naked,

"Nor to suffer from thirst, Nor from the sun's heat."

But Satan whispered evil To him : he said, " O Adam ! Shall I lead thee to The Tree of Eternity And to a kingdom That never decays ? "

"In the result, they both Ate of the tree, and so Their nakedness appeared To them : they began to sew Together, for their covering, Leaves from the Garden : Thus did Adam disobey His Lord, and allow himself To be seduced.

But his Lord chose him (For His Grace) : He turned To him, and gave him guidance.

He said : " Get ye down, Both of you,—all together, From the Garden, with enmity One to another ; but if, As is sure, there comes to you Guidance from Me, whosoever Follows My guidance, will not Lose his way, nor fall Into misery.

" But whosoever turns away From My Message, verily For him is a life narrowed Down, and We shall raise Him up blind on the Day Of Judgment."[35]

These Quranic verses addressed to Adam and Eve in Paradise warned them not to eat from a certain tree, as doing so would make them susceptible to Satan's influence and persecution. By whispering to them, he exposed their vulnerabilities and misled them regarding the forbidden tree, aiming to unveil what was concealed from them. He falsely claimed that Allah ﷻ forbade them from the tree to prevent them from living eternally. This deception underscores Satan's deceptive nature, rooted in his identity as a jinn.

Furthermore, Satan displays arrogance, as illustrated in the Quran, when he declined to prostrate to Adam. This act of prostration was a gesture of acknowledgment, not worship. Satan's arrogance is apparent in his refusal, questioning why he should prostrate to a being formed from clay when he himself was crafted from fire.

In another Quranic verse akin to this, Satan's hubris becomes apparent when queried about his refusal to prostrate before Allah. He retorts, *"I am better than him. You created me from fire, whereas You created him from clay."* The Quran recounts this exchange between Allah and Iblīs.

---

35 Sūra 20: Tā-Hā, 115-124

"(God) said : " O Iblīs ! what prevents thee from Prostrating thyself to one Whom I have created With My hands ? Art thou haughty ? Or art thou one Of the high (and mighty) ones ?"

"(Iblīs) said : " I am better Than he : Thou createdst Me from fire, and him Thou createdst from clay."[36]

This refusal stemmed from a sense of superiority, rejecting the notion of bowing to a being made from inferior material.

Additionally, the Quran advises believers not to be led astray or prevented from the right path by Satan, as he has shown clear enmity towards humanity. Satan's mission, as outlined in the Quran, is solely to invite others to follow him, those who choose to be his followers.

The Prophet Muḥammad ﷺ conveyed that Satan endeavors to sow discord and conflict in various relationships: between father and son, husband and wife, siblings, individuals, groups, and even nations. The prevalence of strained parent-child relationships today reflects the success of Satan's divisive tactics. Parents have often faltered in their duty to raise their children properly, and children are no longer as obedient and loyal as they once were. This breakdown in familial bonds is attributed to Satan's influence, as we have neglected seeking Allah's protection from his harmful machinations.

The corruption and disharmony prevalent in Muslim families, communities, and nations are attributed to the influence of Satan, who seeks to disrupt peace and harmony among people.

---

36 Sūra 38: Sād, 75-76

In the chapter of Surah Yūsuf, Allah ﷻ recounts the tale of Yūsuf and his brothers from beginning to end. It details the conspiracy plotted by his siblings against him, leading to his being cast into a well. Despite their treachery, Allah ﷻ ultimately rescued Yūsuf. After a span of forty years, Yūsuf reflects on this ordeal, acknowledging that it was Satan who sowed discord and animosity between him and his brothers. He expresses gratitude to Allah ﷻ for reconciling them.

Allah ﷻ says:

"And he raised his parents High on the throne (of dignity), And they fell down in prostration, (All) before him. He said : " O my father ! this is The fulfillment of my vision Of old ! God hath made it Come true ! He was indeed Good to me when He Took me out of prison And brought you (all here) Out of the desert, (Even) after Satan had sown Enmity between me and my brothers. Verily my Lord understandeth Best the mysteries of all That He planneth to do. For verily He is full Of knowledge and wisdom."[37]

This verse makes clear that the conflict between Yūsuf and his brothers was instigated by Satan's machinations.

Therefore, islamic teachings emphasize the importance of faith, knowledge, and righteous deeds in overcoming the influence of Satan and his cohorts. Believers are encouraged to cultivate a strong connection with Allah ﷻ through sincere worship, repentance, and adherence to Islamic teachings. Seeking knowledge of the Quran and Sunnah -traditions of the Prophet Muhammad ﷺ- and following the guidance of righteous

---

37 Sūra 12: Yūsuf, 100

scholars are recommended as means of spiritual empowerment and protection against satanic deception.

One of Satan's primary goals is to make us forget the remembrance of Allah ﷻ, neglect our duties towards Him, and overlook the rights of others upon us. When individuals fail to pray, fast, or fulfill their obligations to Allah ﷻ, it's a sign that they have succumbed to Satan's influence. Allah ﷻ describes this in the Quran when He mentions how Satan overpowers people and makes them forget to remember Him.

"Satan's plan is (but) to excite enmity and hatred between you with intoxicants and gambling and hinder you from the remembrance of God and from prayer: will ye not then abstain?"[38]

The verse describes Satan as a clear enemy to humanity. Satan's tactics aim to disrupt our worship, hinder our focus in prayer, impede our studies, isolate us from others, and obstruct us from performing good deeds.

The Quran and prophetic tradition abound with warnings against the schemes of Shaytān and his deceit, urging believers to steadfastly resist them. The following excerpts from the Quran exemplify this guidance:

«O ye who believe ! Follow not Satan's footsteps : If any will follow the footsteps Of Satan, he will (but) command What is shameful and wrong»[39]

In this verse, Allah ﷻ warns, ***"Do not follow the footsteps***

---

38 Sūra 5: Māida, 91

39 Sūra 24: Nūr, 12

of Satan." These "footsteps" represent a series of techniques employed by Satan to lead individuals astray. It's crucial to note that Allah ﷻ doesn't mention "footstep" singular but rather "footsteps" plural, indicating the multifaceted nature of Satan's strategies. If one approach fails, Satan swiftly transitions to another, exploiting vulnerabilities to entice individuals towards wrongdoing. His steps can be categorized into three phases:

1- The pre-action phase, where Satan subtly whispers temptations and desires, planting seeds of doubt and temptation in the mind.

2- The second step occurs during the action itself. Here, Satan employs tactics to dissuade and distract individuals. He instills laziness, creating excuses to deter one from fulfilling their obligations. For instance, when it's time to pray, he may prompt feelings of lethargy, urging one to prioritize sleep or other activities over worship. Additionally, he diverts attention away from important tasks, leading to moments of forgetfulness or distraction, causing individuals to miss appointments or neglect responsibilities, despite making plans or writing reminders. Satan influences forgetfulness, hindering individuals from fulfilling their commitments or duties.

The Prophet Muhammad ﷺ taught us that when we sleep and intend to wake up for prayer, Satan attempts to dissuade us from rising by whispering that it's still time to sleep. He even goes as far as tying knots upon us to keep us in a state of slumber. However, if we resist and wake up, each knot is undone as we take steps to perform ablution (wuḍū) and pray. By doing so, we break free from the lethargy imposed by Satan and become more active and alert throughout the day. On the other hand, if we succumb to laziness and fail to overcome these obstacles, we wake up feeling sluggish and unproductive.

It was narrated that 'Abdullah said:

"Mention was made to the Messenger of Allah (ﷺ) of a man who slept until morning came. He said: 'That is because Satan urinated in his ears.'"[40]

The scholars have disagreed about what is meant by urine here, whether it is the literal meaning or the figurative meaning. Ibn Ḥajar may Allah ﷻ have mercy upon him said in Fatḥ al-Bārī:

"There is a difference of opinion about the urine of the devil, and it was said that it is the real urine; al-Qurṭubī, and others said: This is possible as this is not impossible because it is proven that the devil eats and drinks and marries, so it is possible that he urinates. It was also said that it is a metaphor for the devil blocking the ear of the person who sleeps and does not perform the prayer so that he would not listen to the Dhikr (mention of Allah). It was further said that the devil filled one's hearing with falsehood and prevented his hearing from the Dhikr; and it was said that it is a metaphor for the devil despising him. Moreover, it was said that the devil took hold of him and underestimated him to the point that he considered him as a toilet prepared for urinating in it as it is customary for someone to urinate upon something he disdains."[41]

---

40 Sunan Ibn Majah 1330 : Book 5, Hadith 528

41 https://www.islamweb.net/en/fatwa/239806/meaning-of-the-hadeeth-satan-urinated-in-his-ear

Abū Hurayra reported God's Messenger as saying,

"When one of you goes to sleep the devil ties three knots at the back of his neck, sealing every knot with, 'You have a long night, so sleep'. So if one awakes and mentions God a knot will be loosened, if he performs ablution a knot will be loosened, and if he prays a knot will be loosened, and in the morning he will be active

3- The third aspect involves the encouragement of postponing actions. As the English proverb states, "Postponement is the procrastination of time," indicating that delaying tasks allows time to slip away. Satan tempts individuals to procrastinate, leading them to push important actions into the distant future. This delay steals valuable time and hinders progress. For example, regarding matters like prayer or wearing the hijab, individuals may rationalize delaying these actions, promising to start praying regularly or wear the hijab after they get married, finish their studies, or achieve some other milestone. However, Allah's commands should be followed promptly, without unnecessary delay or hesitation.

However, comprehending these phases is crucial for recognizing and resisting Satan's deception, enabling believers to remain steadfast on the path of righteousness.

The Quran further highlights the enmity of Satan and his tactics, illustrating how he functions to mislead humanity from the right path and the purpose of their existence, which is to worship Allah alone. Allah ﷻ says:

"Lead to destruction those Whom thou canst among them, With thy (seductive) voice ; Make assaults on

them With thy cavalry and thy Infantry ; mutually share With them wealth and children ; And make promises to them." But Satan promises them Nothing but deceit."[42]

He said: "because Thou hast thrown me out of the way lo! I will lie in wait for them on Thy straight way. "Then will I assault them from before them and behind them from their right and their left: nor wilt Thou find in most of them gratitude (for Thy mercies).[4344]

"..so fight ye against the friends of Satan: feeble indeed is the cunning of Satan"[45]

"Then did Satan make them slip from the (garden) and get them out of the state (of felicity) in which they had been. We said: "Get ye down all (ye people) with enmity between yourselves. On earth will be your dwelling place and your means of livelihood for a time."[46]

"The Evil One threatens you with poverty and bids you to conduct unseemly. God promiseth you His forgiveness and bounties and God careth for all and He knoweth all things".[47]

---

42 Sūra 17: Al-Isrā, 64

43 Sūra 7: A'rāf, 16-17

44 Sūra 7: A'rāf,, 27

45 Sūra 4: Nisāa, 76

46 Sūra 2: Baqara, 36

47 Sūra 2: Baqara, 268

"if any take the Evil One for their intimate what a dreadful intimate he is!".[48]

"..I commend her and her offspring to Thy protection from the Evil One the Rejected."[49]

"Secret counsels are only (Inspired) by the Evil One, In order that he may Cause grief to the Believers ; But he cannot harm them In the least, except as God permits ; and on God Let the Believers Put their trust".[50]

In this verse, Allah ﷻ informs the believers that Satan endeavors to sow sorrow and fear in their hearts, irrespective of their faith backgrounds. Satan's goal is to induce distress and anxiety among the believers, despite lacking any power over them. He employs various tactics, including instilling fear of his allies and utilizing jinn, to achieve his objectives. Therefore, it is crucial for believers to remain vigilant against Satan's efforts to disrupt their peace of mind and to seek refuge in Allah from his influence.

Indeed, Satan's efforts extend to enticing disbelief in Allah ﷻ, as outlined in Surah Al-Hashr. When Satan urged humanity to disbelieve, and they succumbed, they expressed fear of Allah's judgment. Allah ﷻ says:

"(Their allies deceived them), Like the Evil One, When he says to man, " Deny God " : but when (Man) denies God, (The Evil One) says, " I am free of thee : I do fear God, The Lord of the Worlds ! "

---

48 Sūra 4: Nisāa, 38

49 Sūra 3: Āl-i-'Imrān, 36

50 Sūra 58: Mujādila, 10

"The end of both will be That they will go Into the Fire, dwelling Therein for ever. Such is the reward Of the wrong-doers."[51]

The Prophet Muhammad ﷺ taught us that when we sleep and intend to wake up for prayer, Satan attempts to dissuade us from rising by whispering that it's still time to sleep. He even goes as far as tying knots upon us to keep us in a state of slumber. However, if we resist and wake up, each knot is undone as we take steps to perform ablution (wuḍū) and pray. By doing so, we break free from the lethargy imposed by Satan and become more active and alert throughout the day. On the other hand, if we succumb to laziness and fail to overcome these obstacles, we wake up feeling sluggish and unproductive. It was narrated that 'Abdullah said:

"Mention was made to the Messenger of Allah (ﷺ) of a man who slept until morning came. He said: 'That is because Satan urinated in his ears.'"[52]

The scholars have disagreed about what is meant by urine here, whether it is the literal meaning or the figurative meaning. Ibn Ḥajar may Allah have mercy upon him said in Fatḥ al-Bārī:

"There is a difference of opinion about the urine of the devil, and it was said that it is the real urine; al-Qurṭubī, and others said: This is possible as this is not impossible because it is proven that the devil eats and drinks and marries, so it is possible that he urinates. It was also said that it is a metaphor for the devil blocking the ear of the person who sleeps and does not perform the prayer so that he would not listen to the Dhikr (mention of Allah). It

---

51 Sūra 59: Hashr, 16-17

52 Sunan Ibn Majah 1330 : Book 5, Hadith 528

was further said that the devil filled one's hearing with falsehood and prevented his hearing from the Dhikr; and it was said that it is a metaphor for the devil despising him. Moreover, it was said that the devil took hold of him and underestimated him to the point that he considered him as a toilet prepared for urinating in it as it is customary for someone to urinate upon something he disdains."[53]

Abū Hurayra reported God's Messenger as saying,

"When one of you goes to sleep the devil ties three knots at the back of his neck, sealing every knot with, 'You have a long night, so sleep'. So if one awakes and mentions God a knot will be loosened, if he performs ablution a knot will be loosened, and if he prays a knot will be loosened, and in the morning he will be active

The Prophet Muḥammad ﷺ also warned against the deceptive tactics of Satan, urging believers to remain vigilant and adhere to the path of righteousness.

It was narrated that Sabrah bin. Abī Fākih said:

"I heard the Messenger of Allah (ﷺ) say: 'the Shayṭān sits in the paths of the son of Adam. He sits waiting for him, in the path to Islam, and he says: Will you accept Islam, and leave your religion, and the religion of your forefathers? But he disobeys him and accepts Islam. Then he sits waiting for him, on the path to emigration, and he says: Will you emigrate and leave behind your land and sky? The one who emigrates

---

53 https://www.islamweb.net/en/fatwa/239806/meaning-of-the-hadeeth-satan-urinated-in-his-ear

is like a horse tethered to a peg. But he disobeys him and emigrates. Then he sits, waiting for him, on the path to Jihad, and he says: Will you fight in Jihad when it will cost you your life and your wealth? You will fight and be killed, and your wife will remarry, and your wealth will be divided. But he disobeys him and fights in Jihad.' The Messenger of Allah (ﷺ) said: 'Whoever does that, then he had a right from Allah, the Mighty and Sublime, that He will admit him to paradise. Whoever is killed, he has a right from Allah, the Mighty and Sublime, that He will admit him to Paradise. If he is drowned, he has a right from Allah that He will admit him to paradise, or whoever is thrown by his mount and his neck is broken, he had a right from Allah that he will admit him to Paradise.'"[54]

Abū Dardā' (May Allah be pleased with him) reported:

«I heard the Messenger of Allah (ﷺ) saying, "If three men in a village or in the desert, make no arrangement for Salat in congregation, Satan must have certainly overcome them. So observe Salat in congregation, for the wolf eats up a solitary sheep that stays far from the flock."[55]

Among the tactics of Satan is to lead believers astray by encouraging innovations and practices that deviate from the teachings of the Quran and Sunnah. Instead of adhering to the established ways of worship as taught by the Prophet Muḥammad ﷺ some may introduce new rituals or modifications to existing

---

54 Sunan an-Nasa'i 3134 : Book 25, Hadith 50,

55 Abu Daud 547, al-Nasai' 847 https://sunnah.com/nasai:3134

ones. However, it's essential to remember that Islam provides clear guidance on how to pray, fast, and practice the faith, as exemplified by the Prophet's teachings.

The Prophet Muḥammad ﷺ emphasized the importance of following his example in worship, stating, **"Pray as you have seen me pray."**[56] Therefore, any act of worship that lacks a basis in the Quran or Sunnah should be regarded with caution, as it may stem from Satan's deception rather than true Islamic teachings.

Satan may tempt individuals to engage in acts of worship for the sake of receiving praise or recognition from others. This can lead to a desire for validation and acknowledgment, causing individuals to seek admiration for their religious deeds. For example, someone may donate a significant sum of money to build a mosque, frequent the mosque regularly, or help others generously, with the underlying intention of gaining praise and admiration from society.

This tendency towards seeking validation can even extend to acts of worship, where individuals may perform prayers or fasting with the intention of being perceived as pious by others. Such actions can become a form of showmanship, where individuals seek approval and commendation for their religious devotion.

Furthermore, individuals may expect gratitude or acknowl-edgment from those they help or support, leading to disappoint-ment or anger if not received. However, true devotion to God should be free from any expectation of reward or recognition from others. Allah emphasizes in the Quran the importance of sincerity and humility in worship, reminding believers that their actions should be solely for the sake of pleasing Him, without

---

56 Ṣaḥīḥ al-Bukhārī 5662, Ṣaḥīḥ Muslim 674, it was narrated by Malik bin Huwayrith

seeking praise or thanks from others. Therefore, it's essential to guard against the temptation of seeking validation or praise for religious deeds and to ensure that our worship is sincerely dedicated to pleasing Allah alone.

Ultimately, it is worth noting that Satan is relentless in his efforts to fulfill his schemes and tactics at any cost, working around the clock without rest. He operates 24 hours a day, 168 hours a week, and a staggering 5,040 hours per month, totaling 60,480 hours per year, during which he tirelessly pursues his goals. Unlike any human worker, he never takes a break, relentlessly engaging in his schemes day and night, even infiltrating dreams with his whisperings and deceptions. Given the fact that Satan is such a tireless entity fully committed to his job, we as believers should not exert any less effort than him regarding protecting ourselves against his misleading. Likewise, we should be fully dedicated to achieving our goals in this world and the hereafter. The Chinese proverb aptly notes that if one wishes to achieve results in their endeavors, they must be as industrious as the devil. This isn't to advocate for adopting his malevolent ways, but rather to emphasize the importance of dedication and hard work in achieving one's goals. Just as the devil is unwavering in his efforts, individuals should approach their tasks with the same level of commitment and diligence, investing their time and energy wholeheartedly to succeed in their endeavors.

THE PROPHET'S ADVICE ON NIGHTTIME PRECAUTIONS AGAINST JINN MISCHIEF

The Prophet Muḥammad ﷺ provided guidance regarding the activities of Jinn during the night. He advised precautions such as closing doors, keeping children indoors, and covering food containers to prevent mischief caused by roaming jinn. Narrated Jābir b. 'Abdullah: Allah's Messenger (ﷺ) said,

"When night falls (or when it is evening), stop your children from going out, for the devils spread out at that time. But when an hour of the night has passed, release them and close the doors and mention Allah's Name, for Satan does not open a closed door. Tie the mouth of your waterskin and mention Allah's Name; cover your containers and utensils and mention Allah's Name. Cover them even by placing something across it, and extinguish your lamps."[57]

Ibn 'Abd al-Barr commenting on the narration, said:

"This is a prophetic tradition enjoined to keep people safe from the devils among mankind and jinn. The Prophet's words 'the devil does not open something closed, and does not untie a water skin,□ consists in his informing about Allah□s favor to His human slaves in that the devil was not given the power to open doors, untie water skins or uncover utensils, and that the devil was deprived of this ability, even though he was given the ability to do what is worse than this, like entering places humans cannot enter»[58]

This highlights the belief in the unseen world and the potential influence of Jinn on human affairs.

---

57 Ṣaḥīḥ al-Bukhārī 5623 : Book 74, Hadith 49

58 Ibn 'Abd al-Barr, al-Istizkar, 8/363

SECTION THREE
THE JINN PHENOMENON IN ISLAMIC THEOLOGY

EXPLORING THEIR NATURE & INFLUENCE

In scholarly terms, Jinn, akin to humans, possess a cognitive construct of free will that may not uniformly align with submission to authority. Their behavioral spectrum encompasses obedience, defiance, amicability, hostility, benevolence, and malevolence towards humanity. The designation "Satan" or "Shayṭān" denotes a sentient entity characterized by disobedience, unmanageability, injurious intent, malevolence, and peril, particularly directed towards humans. Analogously, "Shayāṭīn" signifies a collective of deviant, unruly, obstinate, recalcitrant, unfriendly, harmful, criminal, and demonic entities, acting as proxies of Iblīs.

Both humans and Jinn qualify as "Shayāṭīn" when they manifest traits of malevolence, obstinacy, and non-submission to the divine commands, thereby deviating from the ordained path. The behavioral proclivities of "Shayāṭīn," whether exhibited by humans or Jinn, are not immutable; they can undergo transformation towards obedience and compliance through appropriate guidance, intervention, and training, contingent upon divine will.

The Messenger of Allah ﷺ discerned the constituents of the Jinn community by scrutinizing their inherent disposition, conduct, attributes, outward semblance, and distinguishing features. A tradition (Hadith) elucidates that Jinn assume three distinct forms: one resembling certain members of the Canidae family and reptiles, another traversing the aerial domain imperceptible to the unaided eye, and a third assuming a guise akin to humans. Additionally, other fauna such as scorpions and lizards are also recognized as potential manifestations of Jinn entities.[59]

EXPLORING JINN FACTIONAL DYNAMICS

In the realm of the jinn, as depicted in the Quranic verse, there exist various sects and factions. When a group of Jinn encountered the Prophet Muḥammad ﷺ while he was leading prayers and heard him reciting the Quran, they were struck by its novelty and profoundness. They returned to their people and warned them against polytheism (shirk), affirming the divine

---

59 Farhana Akter, Mar 30, 2024https://fakter-64263.medium.com/your-companions-7e888d027c6e

origin of the Quran and urging belief in its message. The Quran refers to this incident in two chapters:

The first chapter is Sūra 46: Ahqāf:

"Behold, We turned Towards thee a company Of Jinns (quietly) listening To the Qur-ān : when they Stood in the presence Thereof, they said, " Listen In silence ! " When the (reading) Was finished, they returned To their people, to warn (Them of their sins).

"They said, " O our people ! We have heard a Book Revealed after Moses, Confirming what came Before it : it guides (men) To the Truth and To a Straight Path.

" O our people, hearken To the one who invites (You) to God, and believe In him : He will forgive You your faults, And deliver you from A Penalty Grievous.

" If any does not hearken To the one who invites (Us) to God, he cannot Frustrate (God's Plan) on earth, And no protectors can he have Besides God : such men (Wander) in manifest error."[60]

Second chapter is Sūra 72: Jinn, Allah ﷻ says:

"Say : It has been Revealed to me that A company of Jinns Listened (to the Qur-ān). They said, ' We have Really heard a wonderful Recital !

' It gives guidance To the Right, And we have believed therein : We shall not join (in worship) Any (gods) with our Lord.

---

60 Sūra 46: Ahqāf, 29-31

' And exalted is the Majesty Of our Lord : He has Taken neither a wife Nor a son.

' There were some foolish ones Among us, who used To utter extravagant lies Against God ;

' But we do think That no man or spirit Should say aught that is Untrue against God.

'True, there were persons Among mankind who took shelter With persons among the Jinns, But they increased them In folly.

' And they (came to) think As ye thought, that God Would not raise up Any one (to Judgment).

' And we pried into The secrets of heaven ; But we found it filled With stern guards And flaming fires.

' We used, indeed, to sit there In (hidden) stations, to (steal) A hearing ; but any Who listens now Will find a flaming fire Watching him in ambush.

'And we understand not Whether ill is intended To those on earth, Or whether their Lord (Really) intends to guide Them to right conduct.

' There are among us Some that are righteous, And some the contrary : We follow divergent paths.

' But we think that we Can by no means frustrate God throughout the earth, Nor can we frustrate Him By flight.

' And as for us, Since we have listened To the Guidance, we have Accepted it : and any Who believes in his Lord

Has no fear, either Of a short (account) Or of any injustice.

' Amongst us are some That submit their wills (To God), and some That swerve from justice. Now those who submit Their wills—they have Sought out (the path) Of right conduct :

' But those who swerve,— They are (but) fuel For Hell-Fire '—"[61]

According to the verses of this chapter, these Jinn described themselves as comprising different categories, including the righteous (Ṣāliḥūn) and the disobedient (Qāsitūn). They acknowledged the existence of believers, disbelievers, and hypocrites among them. Similarly, they recognized different factions within their community, analogous to human groups such as Ahl al-Sunnah (adherents to the Prophet's tradition) and Ahl al-Ḍalāl (those who deviate from the right path).

Allah ﷻ confirms this diversity among the jinn, stating that those who transgress and do not adhere to His commands will face punishment in Hellfire. This underscores the importance of obedience and adherence to divine guidance, as well as the consequences of deviating from righteousness.

METAMORPHOSIS IN JINN: EXPLORING VERSATILITY AND MYSTIQUE

The world of the Jinn bears similarities to our earthly realm, as described by the Prophet Muḥammad ﷺ. One notable aspect of the jinn's existence is their ability to undergo metamorphosis,

___
61 Sūra 72: Jinn, 1-15

allowing them to transform into various creatures. This capability, known as metamorphosization, grants them the flexibility to take on different forms, whether it be that of a cat, a dog, a human being, or any other creature.

The concept of metamorphosis highlights the versatility and mystical nature of the jinn, emphasizing their supernatural attributes and the intricacies of their existence. According to Islamic teachings, this ability shows jinn's distinct nature and their capacity to interact with the physical and spiritual dimensions of the world.

According to historical accounts narrated by the Prophet Muḥammad ﷺ, during the preparations for the Battle of Badr, an engagement between Muslims and their adversaries, Iblīs, disguised as a human, attended the gathering. He deceitfully assumed the form of a known individual, intending to deceive the Muslims. Pretending to be supportive, he assured them of victory and offered assistance.

However, when the battle commenced and the Muslims assembled on the battlefield, Iblīs witnessed the descent of angels and the presence of Angel Jibrīl. Overwhelmed by fear and recognizing the divine intervention, he fled from the scene. This incident is mentioned in Surah Al-Anfal of the Quran, where Allah ﷻ states that Iblīs saw what the humans did not see, acknowledging his fear of Allah ﷻ and his subsequent flight from the battlefield. Allah ﷻ said:

"Remember Satan made Their (sinful) acts seem Alluring to them, and said : " No one among men Can overcome you this day, While I am near to you " : But when the two forces Came in sight of each other, He

turned on his heels, And said : " Lo ! I am clear Of you ; lo ! I see What ye see not ; Lo ! I fear God ; for God Is strict in punishment."[62]

It was narrated that Ibn ʿAbbās (may Allah be pleased with him) said:

"Iblīs came on the day of Badr bringing a troop of devils with him. I saw him in the form of a man from Banu Mudlij, in the form of Suraaqah ibn Maalik ibn Juʿsham. The Shaytaan said to the mushrikin: No one of mankind can overcome you this day (of the battle of Badr) and verily, I will be your protector. Then when the people had drawn themselves up in battle array, the Messenger of Allah (blessings and peace of Allah be upon him) picked up a handful of dust and threw it in the faces of the mushrikin, and they turned and fled. Jibrīl came to Iblīs and when he saw him, his hand was in the hand of one of the mushrik men. Iblīs pulled his hand away, and turned and fled, he and his party. The man said: O Suraaqah, did you not say that you would protect us? He said: 'Verily! I see what you see not. Verily! I fear Allah for Allah is Severe in punishment.' That was when he saw the angels".[63]

It was was narrated by Mālik b. Anas in al-Muwaṭṭaʾ from

---

62 Sūra 8: Anfāl, 48

63 at-Tabaraani in his Tafsīr (13/7), it was narrated from Ibn ʿAbbaas (may Allah be pleased with him), and there are some reservations about its isnaad, because it is one of the reports narrated by ʿAli ibn Abi Talhah from him. At-Tabaraani narrated in al-Muʿjam al-Kabīr (5/47) from Rifaaʿah ibn Raafiʿ al-Ansaari a report similar to that of Ibn ʿAbbaas, but its isnaad is daʿeef. It includes ʿAbd al-ʿAzeez ibn ʿImraan, who is daʿeef; he was classed as daʿeef by al-Haythami, who gave reasons for that, in Majmaʿ az-Zawaaʾid (6/82)

Ṭalḥa b. 'Ubaydullah b. Karīz, according to which the Messenger of Allah ﷺ said:

"Iblīs is never seen on any day smaller, more humiliated, more defeated and more angry than on the day of 'Arafah, because of what he sees of the descent of mercy and forgiveness for sins, except what he saw on the day of Badr." They said: O Messenger of Allah, what did he see on the day of Badr? He said: "He saw Jibrīl organising the angels."[64]

Additionally, these accounts illustrate the deceptive nature of Iblīs and his ultimate defeat in the face of divine intervention. Despite his initial attempts to mislead the Muslims, he was unable to withstand the manifestation of divine power and withdrew from the confrontation.

Ibn Taymiyyah, asserts that jinn, including the devil, possess the ability to morph or transform into various creatures. This includes instances where they may appear as a black cat, among other forms. He said:

"Jinn can come in the form of black dogs. Similarly they can also come in the form of black cats"[65]

In Fatḥ al-Bārī, 'Umar was asked how can Jinn morph and take a physical structure different from their own? He said they cannot do that without the help of the magicians amongst the jinn. So if you see one, make the Ādhān, because they flee when they hear it.

---

64 This a mursal hadeeth that was narrated by Maalik in al-Muwatta' (944) from Talhah ibn 'Ubaydullah ibn Kareez, it strengthens the meaning of the previous report of ibn Abbaas.

65 Majmu 'ul Fatawa, vol. 19 pg. 52

They can inhabit idols and objects and in order for the person to believe they have real power.

However, it's important to note that encountering a black cat or dog should not prompt harmful actions, such as throwing stones or killing them. Rather, Ibn Taymiyyah emphasizes the need for caution and understanding, recognizing that such creatures may simply be natural animals and not necessarily man-ifestations of malevolent entities. This concept of metamorphosis aligns with the teachings of the Prophet Muḥammad ﷺ, who also spoke of the jinn's ability to change forms. Therefore, while acknowledging the supernatural capabilities of jinn, it's essential to approach such encounters with wisdom and discernment, refraining from unnecessary harm or superstition.

The incident from Ṣaḥīḥ al-Bukhārī involves Abū Hurayra, a companion of the Prophet Muḥammad ﷺ, who was guarding the Muslim treasury. Over three consecutive nights, Abū Hurayra apprehended a man attempting theft. On the third night, the man advised Abū Hurayra to recite Ayat al-Kursi repeatedly for protection from evil forces, including Jinn and Satan.

Abū Hurayra reported this encounter to the Prophet Muḥammad ﷺ, who confirmed the truth in the man's statement despite labeling him as a liar.

Abū Hurayra (May Allah be pleased with him) reported:

The Messenger of Allah (ﷺ) put me in charge of charity of Ramaḍān (Ṣadaqat al-Fitr). Somebody came to me and began to take away some food-stuff. I caught him and said, "I must take you to the Messenger of Allah (ﷺ)." He said, "I am a needy man with a large family, and so I have a pressing need." I let him go. When I saw

the Messenger of Allah (ﷺ) next morning, he asked me, "O Abū Hurayra! What did your captive do last night?" I said, "O Messenger of Allah! He complained of a pressing need and a big family. I felt pity for him so I let him go." He (ﷺ) said, "He told you a lie and he will return." I was sure, according to the saying of the Messenger of Allah (ﷺ) that he would return. I waited for him. He sneaked up again and began to steal food-stuff from the Ṣadaqah. I caught him and said; "I must take you to the Messenger of Allah (ﷺ)." He said, "Let go of me, I am a needy man. I have to bear the expenses of a big family. I will not come back." So I took pity on him and let him go. I went at dawn to the Messenger of Allah (ﷺ) who asked me, "O Abū Hurayra! What did your captive do last night?" I replied, "O Messenger of Allah! He complained of a pressing want and the burden of a big family. I took pity on him and so I let him go." He (ﷺ) said, "He told you a lie and he will return." (That man) came again to steal the food-stuff. I arrested him and said, "I must take you to the Messenger of Allah (ﷺ), and this is the last of three times. You promised that you would not come again but you did." He said, "Let go of me, I shall teach you some words with which Allah may benefit you." I asked, "What are those words?" He replied, "When you go to bed, recite Ayat-ul- Kursi (2:255) for there will be a guardian appointed over you from Allah, and Satan will not be able to approach you till morning." So I let him go. Next morning the Messenger of Allah (ﷺ) asked me, "What did your prisoner do last night." I answered, "He promised to teach me some words which he claimed will benefit me before Allah. So I let him go." The Messenger of Allah (ﷺ) asked, "What are those words that he taught you?" I said, "He told me: 'When you go to bed, recite Ayat- ul-Kursi from the beginning to the end i.e.,[Allah! none has the right to be worshipped but He, the Ever Living, the One Who sustains and protects all that exists. Neither slumber nor sleep overtakes Him. To Him belongs whatever is in the heavens and whatever is on the earth. Who is he that can intercede with Him except with His Permission? He knows what happens to them (His creatures) in this world, and what will happen to them in the Hereafter. And they will never compass anything of His Knowledge except that which He wills. His Kursi encompasses the heavens and the earth, and preserving them does not fatigue Him. And He is the Most High, the Most Great].' (2:255). He added: 'By reciting it, there will be a guardian appointed over you from Allah who will protect you during the night, and Satan will not be able to come near you until morning'." The Messenger of Allah (ﷺ) said, "Verily, he has told you the truth though he is a liar. O Abū Hurayra! Do you know with whom you were speaking for the last three nights?" I said, "No." He (ﷺ) said, "He was Shayṭān (Satan)."[66]

This illustrates the transformative abilities of jinn, as the man was able to disguise his true identity and appear as a human while attempting theft. The Prophet Muḥammad ﷺ affirmed the efficacy of Ayat al-Kursi as a means of spiritual protection against malevolent entities, highlighting its significance in warding off evil.

---

66 Ṣaḥīḥ al-Bukhārī 5010, Book 66, Hadith 32 https://sunnah.com/riyadussalihin:1020

Abū al-Sāʾib, the freed slave of Hishām b. Zuhra, said that he visited Abū Saʿīd al-Khudrī in his house, (and he further) said:

"I found him saying his prayer, so I sat down waiting for him to finish his prayer when I heard a stir in the bundles (of wood) lying in a comer of the house. I looked towards it and found a snake. I jumped up in order to kill it, but he (Abū Saʿīd al-Khudrī) made a gesture that I should sit down. So I sat down and as he finished (the prayer) he pointed to a room in the house and said: Do you see this room? I said: Yes. He said: There was a young man amongst us who had been newly wedded. We went with Allah's Messenger ﷺ (to participate in the Battle) of Trench when a young man in the midday used to seek permission from Allah's Messenger ﷺ to return to his family. One day he sought permission from him and Allah's Messenger ﷺ (after granting him the permission) said to him: Carry your weapons with you for I fear the tribe of Qurayẓa (may harm you). The man carried the weapons and then came back and found his wife standing between the two doors. He bent towards her smitten by jealousy and made a dash towards her with a spear in order to stab her. She said: Keep your spear away and enter the house until you see that which has made me come out. He entered and found a big snake coiled on the bedding. He darted with the spear and pierced it and then went out having fixed it in the house, but the snake quivered and attacked him and no one knew which of them died first, the snake or the young man. We came to Allah's Apostle ﷺ and made a mention to him and said: Supplicate to Allah that that (man) may be brought back to life. Thereupon he

said: Ask forgiveness for your companion and then said: There are in Medina Jinns who have accepted Islam, so when you see any one of them, pronounce a warning to it for three days, and if they appear before you after that, then kill it for that is a devil."[67]

In this narration, the Prophet Muḥammad ﷺ advised us against causing harm to creatures, as they could potentially be Jinn transforming into the form of these creatures. This guidance makes clear the importance of showing compassion and kindness towards all living beings, as they may not always be what they appear to be.

This narration is a story of a newlywed man who, during his honeymoon, attended congregational prayers at the mosque. Upon returning home, he found a snake in the room. Enraged, he attempted to kill it with a sword. However, the outcome was uncertain, as narrated in Ṣaḥīḥ al-Bukhārī, whether the man or the snake's head was struck first, resulting in the man's demise. The Prophet ﷺ emphasized caution when encountering potentially harmful creatures like snakes or insects, advising to warn them before attempting to kill them. Such beings could be Jinn or devils, capable of morphing into other forms. Hence, hasty actions should be avoided.

The Prophet ﷺ, advised that the man should have knocked on the door and warned the snake to leave, as the Jinn would heed his warning. This indicates a crucial point. While some might dismiss such teachings as superstition, it's essential to discern between authentic Islamic teachings from the Quran and Sunnah and mere superstition. We meticulously adhere to sound

---

67 Sahih Muslim 2236a (Book 39, Hadith 190)

prophetic traditions with reliable chains of narration, steering clear of weak narrations that could lead us astray. Safeguarding our creed ('Aqīda) demands such discernment and care.

THE PROPHET ﷺ WITNESSING THE JINN

According to Ṣaḥīḥ al-Bukhārī, a significant event occurred during one of the Prophet Muḥammad's prayers. While praying one night, a devil attempted to whisper into his ears, disrupting his concentration and almost causing him to abandon the prayer. In response, the Prophet Muḥammad ﷺ seized the devil and intended to chastise it severely. However, he refrained from doing so, remembering the invocation made by Prophet Solomon (peace be upon him). Solomon had asked Allah ﷻ for a kingdom that would be exclusively his, not to be shared by any other person, be it a prophet, messenger, or anyone else after him. Reflecting on this, the Prophet Muḥammad ﷺ chose not to display the devil publicly, out of respect for the sanctity of prayer and Solomon's supplication for an exclusive kingdom.

"Narated By Abū Hurayra : The Prophet once offered the prayer and said, "Satan came in front of me and tried to interrupt my prayer, but Allah gave me an upper hand on him and I choked him. No doubt, I thought of tying him to one of the pillars of the mosque till you get up in the morning and see him. Then I remembered the statement of Prophet Solomon, 'My Lord ! Bestow on me a kingdom such as shall not belong to any other after me.' Then Allah made him (Satan) return with his head down (humiliated)."[68]

---

68 Ṣaḥīḥ al-Bukhārī Volume 2, Book 22, Hadith Number 301. https://hadithcollection.com/sahihbukhari/sahih-bukhari-book-22-actions-while-praying/sahih-bukhari-volume-

SECTION FOUR:
DISCERNING DECEPTION

THE DANGER OF EXPLOITING SUPERNATURAL FEATS/MIRACLES (KARĀMĀT) IN ISLAM

Indeed, Jinn possess the ability to perform extraordinary feats or miracles (Karāmāt) at the behest of deviant individuals who seek to deceive and mislead others. These individuals, often characterized by their deviation from the right path and their exploitation of the vulnerable or simple-minded, may use such feats to assert their superiority or gain influence over others.

002-book-022-hadith-number-301

The Prophet Muḥammad ﷺ warned against such individuals, emphasizing that they use these feats as tools for deception and manipulation. By exploiting the vulnerabilities of others and presenting themselves as possessing supernatural powers, they lead people astray from the truth and divert them from the path of righteousness.

In Islamic teachings, it's essential for believers to exercise discernment and critical thinking, avoiding being misled by individuals who use deceptive tactics to advance their own agendas.

Imam al-Shāfiʿī provides valuable insight into discerning the authenticity of individuals who claim to possess miraculous powers or divine favor. He advises against blindly believing in such individuals solely based on the display of extraordinary feats. Instead, he emphasizes the importance of observing how a person's life ends, particularly the words they utter at the moment of death.

According to Imam al-Shāfiʿī, the true measure of a person's righteousness lies in their adherence to the fundamental declaration of faith: *"There is no god but Allah, and Muḥammad is the Messenger of Allah" (la ilaha illallah Muḥammad Rasulullah)*. If a person, regardless of their claimed miracles or spiritual status, affirms this declaration at the time of death, it signifies a positive and faithful conclusion to their life.

Imam al-Ghazzālī, in his renowned work "Iḥyāʾ ʿUlūm al-Dīn" provides valuable guidance on discerning between genuine spiritual experiences and deceptive phenomena. He warns against blindly attributing supernatural actions, such as a person floating over oceans without sinking, to divine favor. Instead, he cautions that such occurrences are often the work of Satan, intended to deceive and mislead observers.

This advice indicates the importance of exercising discernment and critical thinking when encountering seemingly miraculous events. Rather than being swayed by extraordinary displays, believers are encouraged to assess the spiritual authenticity of individuals based on their adherence to Islamic principles and values.

THE CONNECTION BETWEEN SUPERSTITIONS AND JINN WHISPERINGS

Superstitious beliefs vary across cultures, yet there are significant similarities among them. For instance, in some African cultures, people refrain from borrowing items from neighbors at night or avoid visiting certain places after dark due to fear of jinn. Such whispers from the Jinn can instill unnecessary fear and instability in people's lives. These beliefs often stem from myths and unfounded fears rather than Islamic teachings.

It's important for believers to distinguish between genuine Islamic teachings and cultural superstitions. Islam encourages rationality, critical thinking, and reliance on authentic sources of knowledge. Instead of succumbing to baseless fears, Muslims should seek guidance from the Quran and Sunnah to navigate life's challenges and uphold their faith with confidence and clarity.

The Prophet Muḥammad ﷺ warned against the dangers of instability caused by whisperings and delusions (waswasa) from Satan. Such whispers can lead to doubt and anxiety, disrupting the peace of mind and interfering with daily activities, including prayer and cleanliness rituals.

The Prophet Muḥammad ﷺ taught us that the whispers and delusions (waswasa) instigated by Satan often occur during moments of extreme emotion, such as happiness, sadness, or fear. Additionally, these whispers may intensify when one loses control of their temper and becomes angry. During such vulnerable moments, individuals are more susceptible to being influenced by negative forces.

To combat these whispers and protect oneself from falling into Satan's trap, the Prophet Muḥammad ﷺ provided practical techniques. When feeling overwhelmed by anger or other emotions, seeking refuge in Allah by saying "A'udhu billahi minash-Shayṭān ir-rajim" (I seek refuge in Allah from Satan, the accursed) can help ward off Satanic influences. Following this, engaging in acts of remembrance (adhkār) such as saying "Astagh-firullah" (I seek forgiveness from Allah) or "Subhanallah" (Glory be to Allah) can further strengthen one's spiritual defenses.

Additionally, Islamic tradition acknowledges the existence of a qarīn, a type of Jinn or demon, assigned to accompany individuals throughout their lives. This qarīn remains with a person from birth until death, influencing their thoughts and actions. While angels encourage righteousness and good deeds, the qarīn may tempt individuals to engage in sinful behavior.

By consistently practicing these remembrances and seeking refuge in Allah during moments of vulnerability, Muslims can fortify themselves against the whispers of Satan and maintain control over their thoughts and actions.

THE RELATIONSHIP BETWEEN MAGICIANS AND JINN

The Prophet Muḥammad ﷺ warned against the practice of magic (Sihr) and its association with the devil. Magic relies on the assistance of Satan and his minions to achieve its effects, making it inherently sinful and contrary to the teachings of Islam. Those who engage in magic are considered to be distant from the path of Allah and are not to be trusted.

The Prophet Muḥammad ﷺ emphasized the severity of seeking the help of magicians or fortune-tellers, stating that the prayers of individuals who resort to such practices will not be accepted for a period of 40 days. This stern warning underscores the gravity of involving oneself in acts of magic or seeking guidance from those who claim supernatural powers.

Furthermore, the Prophet Muḥammad ﷺ declared that involvement in magic constitutes disbelief in the revelations of Allah and the teachings of the Quran.

The Jinn or the devil aids magicians primarily when they engage in acts of shirk, or associating partners with Allah ﷻ. Magicians who commit shirk become spiritually defiled and distance themselves from the guidance and protection of Allah ﷻ. As a result, they become vulnerable to manipulation and influence by the Jinn or the devil.

Magicians often undergo rituals and practices that involve maintaining a state of impurity, neglecting acts of worship such as prayer, and disregarding the remembrance of Allah ﷻ. The Jinn are attracted to such impurity and filth, and they find favor with individuals who exhibit these characteristics.

In exchange for their allegiance and assistance, the Jinn fulfill the requests and desires of the magician. They summon other jinn, particularly the younger and weaker ones, to carry out various tasks and operations, including performing acts of magic. By obeying the commands of the magician, these Jinn enable the practitioner to achieve their goals and fulfill their desires through magical means.

The Prophet Muḥammad ﷺ warned against involvement in magic and emphasized the severe consequences of engaging in such practices. Muslims are urged to uphold faith in Allah ﷻ alone and to avoid associating with acts of shirk, which can lead to spiritual corruption and deviation from the path of righteousness. Instead, believers are encouraged to seek protection and guidance from Allah ﷻ and to rely on His mercy and blessings in all aspects of life.

Indeed, magicians often seek personal items or remnants of individuals to use in their rituals and spells. These items, such as hair, clothing, or personal belongings, are believed to contain the spiritual essence or energy of the person. Magicians use these items to perform rituals aimed at exerting control over the individual or influencing their thoughts and actions.

RULING ON SEEKING THE HELP OF THE JINN IN ISLAM

Seeking the help and assistance of the Jinn is strictly prohibited, as stated in the Quran. Allah ﷻ emphasizes this by saying:

"True, there were persons Among mankind who

took shelter With persons among the Jinns, But they increased them In folly."[69]

Ibn 'Abbās, explaining the verse, said:

"in the pre-Islamic days of ignorance when the Arabs had to spend a night in some uninhabited, desolate valley, they would shout out: We seek refuge of the jinn, who is owner of this valley. In other traditions of the pre-Islamic ignorance also the same thing has been reported frequently. For example, if in a place they ran short of water and fodder, the wandering Bedouins would send one of their men to some other place to see if water and fodder were available; and when they reached the new site under his direction, they would shout out before they halted to pitch the camp: We seek refuge of the sustainer of this valley so that we may live here in peace from every calamity. They believed that every un-inhabited place was under the control of one or another Jinn and if someone stayed there without seeking his refuge, the Jinn would either himself trouble the settlers, or would let others trouble them. These believing Jinn are referring to this very thing. They meant that when man, the vicegerent of the earth, started fearing them without any reason, and started seeking their refuge instead of God's, it caused their people to become even more arrogant, haughty and wicked, and they became even more fearless and bold in adopting error and disbelie".[70]

Seeking the assistance of the Jinn in specific matters, this

---

69 Sūra 72: Jinn, 6

70 https://myislam.org/surah-jinn/ayat-6/

concept has been thoroughly elucidated by Ibn Taymiyyah, who stated the following:

"What is meant here is that the relationship between the Jinn and humans may be of different types. If a human instructs the Jinn to do what Allah and His Messenger have enjoined of worshipping Allah alone and obeying His Prophet, and also instructs people to do that, then he is one of the close friends of Allah, and is also one of the heirs and deputies of the Messenger. The one who asks the Jinn to do permissible things for him, just as he asks humans to do permissible things for him, such as instructing them to do what they should do and telling them not to do things that are forbidden to them, and asking them to do permissible tasks for him, then he is like the kings who do such things. This applies if we assume that he is one of the close friends of Allah, may He be glorified and exalted, so the best thing that we can say about him is that he is one of the close friends of Allah in a general sense, just as there were prophet-kings as well as messenger-slaves, like Sulayman and Yūsuf who held positions of worldly authority in contrast to Ibrahim, Musa, 'Isa and Muḥammad (blessings and peace of Allah be upon them all). As for the one who asks the Jinn to do things that Allah and His Messenger have forbidden, whether that has to do with matters of shirk, or killing one whose life is protected according to Islamic law, or transgressing against people in ways other than killing them, such as causing them to fall sick or to forget knowledge, and other transgressions, or causing them to commit immoral actions, such as bringing to a person someone who will demand that of him – in all these cases he has sought their help to commit sin and transgression.

Moreover, if he seeks their help to commit acts of disbelief, he is a disbeliever; if he seeks their help to commit sin, he is a sinner; he is either an evildoer or he is a sinner but not an evildoer. If he does not have proper knowledge of Islamic teachings and he seeks their help in a manner that he thinks is like performing miracles (Karāmāt) for him, such as seeking their help to go for Hajj, or to make him fly when listening to innovated religious songs, or to carry him to 'Arafat, when he does not do Hajj as prescribed in Islam and as enjoined by Allah and His Messenger, or to carry him from one city to another, and the like, then in this case he is deceived and they have tricked him."[71]

RULING ON SUMMONING SPIRITS OR SOULS IN ISLAM

The practice of seeking communication with deceased individuals through summoning Jinn is considered a form of shirk, or associating partners with Allah, which is strictly prohibited in Islam. The Prophet Muḥammad ﷺ warned against engaging in such practices, emphasizing that those who do so risk being condemned to hellfire.

"What those who promote the summoning of spirits or souls claim is an example of the Jinn toying with humans."[72] The soul is one of the matters of the unseen, knowledge of which Allah, may He be glorified and exalted, has kept to

---

71 Majmu' al-Fatawa, 11/307-309, https://dorar.net/en/aqadia/

72 See: 'Abd al-Karim 'Ubaydat: 'Alam al-Jinn fi Daw' al-Kitab wa'l-Sunnah, p. 447; 'Ali al'Ubaydi: al-Mawsu'ah al-Shamilah li Madhhab al-Ruhiyyah al-Hadithah wa Tahdir al-Arwah, 2/604.

Himself, so it is not right to indulge in such matters except on the basis of textual evidence."[73]

UNDERSTANDING POSSESSION: CATEGORIES, SYMPTOMS, AND SPIRITUAL GUIDANCE IN ISLAM

As for possession, Ibn al-Qayyim highlights two categories: voluntary and involuntary. Voluntary possession is attributed to divine permission due to the individual's sins, such as shirk (associating partners with Allah ﷻ), neglect of prayers, or engaging in immoral behavior. In such cases, Allah ﷻ may allow a Jinn to possess the person as a form of punishment or trial.

On the other hand, involuntary possession is caused by magicians who manipulate Jinn to harm others. This type of possession is condemned in Islam, as it involves unjust manipulation and harm inflicted upon individuals through magical practices.

Before discussing the symptoms, it's crucial to rule out any physical or mental abnormalities such as hysteria. Once that's confirmed, if you experience seeing or hearing things that others don't, it could indicate something spiritual within you. This isn't akin to Hollywood tales; it's a reality that requires attention. If you identify with any of the following symptoms, seek assistance from a knowledgeable individual, such as a Shaykh, and have Quranic recitation performed for you:

If you notice symptoms of split personalities, where you feel like someone else with a different history or biography, it could indicate possession by a jinn. Similarly, if you experience

---

73 Majmu' Fatawa Ibn Baz, 3/311-313, https://dorar.net/en/aqadia/41

sensations like something moving under your skin, seeking help from a knowledgeable individual like a Shaykh and having Quranic recitation performed for you is advised.

Chronic headaches, such as migraines, can also be considered a symptom suggesting susceptibility to possession or actual possession by a jinn. If you or someone you know experiences persistent and severe headaches, it's wise to seek guidance from a knowledgeable individual and consider having Quranic recitation performed for relief and protection.

Rapid mood swings, where one moment you're angry and the next you're laughing, can also indicate susceptibility to possession by a jinn. This vulnerability is often observed in environments where worship of Allah is not prevalent. Those who are not engaged in spiritual activities, fail to consistently read the Holy Quran, neglect self-purification, and disregard Allah's commandments are particularly at risk. Religious scholars emphasize the importance of adhering to spiritual practices as a means of protection against possession.

If you find yourself prone to cursing and being absent-minded, where you feel detached from your surroundings or conversations, it could indicate vulnerability to possession by a demon. In such moments, seek refuge by saying "astaghfirullah" (I seek forgiveness from Allah) or "subhanallah" (glory be to Allah). Additionally, I'll mention the treatment for this condition, God willing (inshallah).

Those who experience difficulty sleeping or have fragmented sleep patterns, where they wake up frequently during the night, are also susceptible to demonic influence. This vulnerability is exacerbated by nightmares, where one dreams of being chased or attacked by various creatures or individuals. To safeguard against such influences, it's crucial to remember and mention Allah before going to bed. Performing ablution (wuḍū), saying "subhanallah" (glory be to Allah), and "astaghfirullah" (I seek forgiveness from Allah) are recommended actions. Following these practices diligently can provide protection, God willing (inshallah).

Instances of possession by Jinn are recognized in Islamic tradition, and exorcism rituals are prescribed to alleviate such afflictions. These rituals typically involve recitation of Quranic verses, prayers, and supplications seeking divine protection and intervention. Allah ﷻ says:

«Those who devour usury will not stand except as stands one whom the Evil One by his touch hath driven to madness».[74]

However, it is important to note that the Prophet Muḥammad ﷺ taught that humans possess a certain level of authority and power over the jinn. While the Jinn may instill fear in some individuals, particularly those who are susceptible to possession due to their vulnerability or lack of faith, believers are encouraged to rely on their faith in Allah and seek protection from Him.

The Prophet Muḥammad ﷺ also provided guidance for such situations. He instructed on the appropriate actions to take, including the use of prescribed remedies and seeking spiritual healing through exorcism

The process of treating a person believed to be possessed by a

---

74 Sūra 2: Baqara, 275

demon, jinn, or Satan in Islam follows a methodological approach established by Sharīʿa law.

In Christianity, the methodology of exorcism differs, but it's crucial to note that the Islamic approach is distinct. In Islam, the foundation of exorcism is firmly rooted in the avoidance of associating partners with Allah (shirk). This is because if the person conducting the exorcism relies on the Jinn for assistance, they risk committing shirk. Similarly, if the individual being cured continues to seek help from the Jinn after being cured, they also fall into the sin of shirk. Therefore, the Islamic method of exorcism ensures adherence to monotheism and avoids any association with beings other than Allah ﷻ.

RUQYA: THE ISLAMIC PRACTICE OF SPIRITUAL HEALING AND

There's a practice called Ruqya in Islam, which involves reciting Quranic verses and chapters on the affected person. The recitation spans from Surah Al-Fatiha to the end of Surah Al-Nasr, encompassing the entire Quran. Any Quranic verse or chapter recited on the person is believed to facilitate their exorcism from the perceived possession. This methodology, as instructed by the Prophet Muḥammad, peace be upon him, serves as a means of spiritual healing and protection.

Distinguishing between physical illness, psychiatric illness, and possession by a Jinn can be discerned through the reaction of the affected person to the Quranic recitation. If the individual reacts strongly, such as shouting, screaming, or displaying discomfort when Quranic verses are recited, it suggests potential possession. However, if there's no reaction or aversion to the

Quranic recitation, it indicates a physical or mental illness. In such cases, seeking medical assistance is necessary, as the person's condition is unrelated to possession and requires appropriate treatment from healthcare professionals.

If a person is believed to have been affected by magic, reciting Quranic verses on them may induce vomiting as a reaction. This involuntary response can be a sign of the presence of magic.

In cases where sorcery is suspected, magicians may utilize two methods: tying knots or using the individual's external remains such as hair. To counteract these effects, the remnants must be disposed of, as the Prophet instructed, or Quranic recitation can be performed as a means of treatment, God willing (in Shā Allah).

Certainly, it's crucial for the person reciting the Quran, the "Rāqī" to be free from associating partners with Allah (shirk). If the reciter is engaging in shirk, they wouldn't be able to effectively treat others. They must ensure their worship is solely directed to Allah ﷻ. Additionally, it's important to eliminate any environments or factors that might attract or facilitate the presence of jinn. This includes removing any idolatrous objects or practices that could create a conducive environment for jinn. Creating a pure and spiritually conducive atmosphere is essential for effective treatment.

The Prophet ﷺ prohibited the presence of pictures in places where the Quran is recited, as this could attract jinn. When it comes to reciting Quranic verses for exorcism, there's no specific prescription regarding the number of repetitions or which verses to recite. Any Quranic verse and any number of repetitions are effective, God willing (inshallah). There's no need for a specific sequence or number of recitations; the recitation of any Quranic verse is beneficial for protection and healing.

Regarding the specifics of Ruqya and its mechanisms, a comprehensive explanation of its steps and methods will be provided in the final section of the book, which discusses the treatment of magic.

VICTORIOUS AGAINST DECEPTION: TACTICS TO COMBAT SATAN'S INFLUENCE

To overcome Satan's interference, we must strengthen our connection with Allah ﷻ and seek His guidance and protection. This involves cultivating taqwā (God-consciousness), regularly reciting Quranic verses for protection, performing acts of worship with sincerity, such as prayer and supplication, and seeking beneficial knowledge that aligns with Islamic teachings.

If one finds arrogance within themselves, characterized by looking down upon others, disrespecting them, or holding oneself in high regard, it is attributed to the influence of Satan, as the Prophet Muḥammad ﷺ warned. This arrogance fluctuates, diminishing when Allah ﷻ is mentioned and increasing when He is not. The Prophet ﷺ taught that reciting the Ādhān causes Satan to flee from the mosque, passing wind, but he returns after the Ādhān concludes. Similarly, during the iqamah, Satan flees again, as narrated by Abū Hurayra that the Messenger of Allah (ﷺ) said:

"When Satan hears the call to prayer, he turns back and breaks the wind so as not to hear the call being made, but when the call is finished he turns round and distracts (the minds of those who pray), and when

he hears the Iqama, he again runs away so as not to hear its voice and when it subsides, he comes back and distracts (the minds of those who stand for prayer)".[75]

Amidst the array of satanic tactics and attempts to mislead believers, it's crucial to remember that Satan's deception is incomparable to Allah's guidance and protection. Allah emphasizes the weakness of Satan's deception by stating its feebleness, **"feeble indeed is the cunning of Satan"**[76]. thus highlighting its inherent frailty and inevitable failure. Allah warns of its significance, indicating its potency and potential impact.

Allah ﷻ reminds us in the Quran that those who prioritize worldly pleasures over spiritual growth will find themselves in Hell, while those who fear their Lord and restrain themselves from sinful desires will be rewarded with Paradise.

So, how do we engage in this struggle? **Firstly**, by cultivating love for Allah in our hearts and making His presence a vibrant aspect of our lives. **Secondly**, by nurturing a deep sense of awe and reverence for Allah, recognizing His authority and power. **Thirdly,** by developing a strong will and determination to resist temptation and adhere to Allah's commandments. And fithly, by acquiring knowledge. As it's been said, "One person with understanding is harder on Satan than a thousand worshippers." This highlights the significance of knowledge in combating the schemes of Satan.

Indeed, the struggle against one's soul is a profound journey, as exemplified by the scholar who devoted 20 years to this endeavor. Through this struggle, one experiences the profound sweetness

---

75 Sahih Muslim 389a : Book 4, Hadith 19

76 Sūra 4: Nisāa, 76

of worshiping Allah, which serves as a source of motivation and spiritual fulfillment.

In conclusion, I want to emphasize that much has been discussed by scholars and within Islam about the devil, and the consensus is clear: it is evil, a tempter, intelligent, and relentless in its pursuit to lead us astray. However, it's crucial to recognize that we hold the power to restrain ourselves from its influence through prayer and adherence to Allah's guidance.

I based this lecture on the Quran to provide insight into Islamic teachings, while also drawing from other scriptures to offer a broader perspective.

As stated in the Quran, **"And those who strive In Our (Cause),—We will Certainly guide them To Our Paths: For verily God Is with those Who do right"**.[77]

---

77 Sūra 29: Ankabūt, 69

CHAPTER 02

BLACK MAGIC: CURES AND PROTECTION

SECTION ONE:
UNVEILING THE PROHIBITION OF MAGIC IN ISLAM: UNDERSTANDING ITS BASIS IN AQIDAH AND DIVINE DECREE

DELIVERED	21st of March, 2016 Peace Conference Scandinavia (organized by IslamNet)

In Islam, magic, horoscopes, fortune-telling, palm reading—anything associated with these practices— are unequivocally condemned and prohibited. This stems from the fundamental belief that only Allah ﷻ knows the unseen. The future, its mysteries, are solely within His knowledge. This conviction is profound, as evidenced by historical actions; during 'Umar's era, he ordered the punishment of all practitioners of magic. Before we transition to our main topic, let's revisit some foundational points pertinent to Aqidah.

Firstly, it's crucial to understand that no one possesses knowledge of the future except Allah subhanahu wa ta'ala. This truth is emphasized in Sūra 7: A'rāf, where Allah states,

"I have no power over any good or harm to myself except as God willeth. If I had knowledge of the unseen I should have multiplied all good and no evil should have touched me I am but a warner and a bringer of glad tidings to those who have faith."[78]

This verse unequivocally asserts that the future is solely known to Allah ﷻ.

Secondly, magic and any resulting harm are ultimately under the decree of Allah ﷻ. His dominion cannot be overpowered by anyone or anything. Therefore, everything that occurs in this world happens by the permission of Allah ﷻ. However, it's crucial to differentiate between Allah's universal will and His legislative will. While Allah ﷻ may allow magic to occur, He neither commands nor approves of it.

Therefore, having this belief firmly entrenched in one's heart provides assurance that magic cannot inflict harm. It's essential to recognize that any harm resulting from magic occurs only with Allah's permission.

78 Sūra 7: A'rāf, Verse 188

"But they could not thus harm anyone except by God's permission"[79]

Thirdly, another crucial point to understand, as highlighted in the Holy Quran, is that no calamity afflicts us on earth or within ourselves except as it is written in a preordained book before it comes into existence. Allah's decree encompasses all, and He brings things into existence effortlessly. This understanding is pivotal as we navigate life's trials and tribulations.

On the authority of Abū 'Abbās 'Abdullah b. 'Abbās (may Allah be pleased with him) who said:

"One day I was behind the Prophet (peace and blessings of Allah be upon him) [riding on the same mount] and he said, "O young man, I shall teach you some words [of advice]: Be mindful of Allah and Allah will protect you. Be mindful of Allah and you will find Him in front of you. If you ask, then ask Allah [alone]; and if you seek help, then seek help from Allah [alone]. And know that if the nation were to gather together to benefit you with anything, they would not benefit you except with what Allah had already prescribed for you. And if they were to gather together to harm you with anything, they would not harm you except with what Allah had already prescribed against you. The pens have been lifted and the pages have dried." It was related by at-Tirmidhi, who said it was a good and sound hadeeth. Another narration, other than that of Tirmidhi, reads: Be mindful of Allah, and you will find Him in front of you. Recognize and

---

79 Sūra 2: Baqara, Verse 102

acknowledge Allah in times of ease and prosperity, and He will remember you in times of adversity. And know that what has passed you by [and you have failed to attain] was not going to befall you, and what has befallen you was not going to pass you by. And know that victory comes with patience, relief with affliction, and hardship with ease".

Indeed, the phrase *"The pens have been lifted and the pages have dried"* refers to the unchangeable nature of Allah's decree, as it is inscribed on the sacred tablet. This reaffirms Allah's divine will and brings peace and tranquility to believers, knowing that everything is decreed by Allah ﷻ. It illustrates the immutable nature of Allah's decree, emphasizing that once ordained, events cannot be altered. Every detail is meticulously recorded in Allah's Book, and nothing happens except according to His will. This profound understanding strengthens the belief in divine predestination and the absolute sovereignty of Allah ﷻ.

The Prophet Muḥammad ﷺ imparted invaluable wisdom to his companions, highlighting the concept that whatever happens to a person was destined to occur, and whatever misses them was never meant to happen. This indicates the belief in divine decree and encourages acceptance of Allah's will with patience and faith.

Fourthly, it's important to acknowledge the possibility of the evil eye[80] and its potential effects. Sometimes, what may begin as the evil eye can escalate into a belief of demonic possession or influence by jinn, eventually leading to accusations of magic. Understanding this progression is crucial.

---

80 For a deeper understanding of the evil eye, I recommend referring to "Exploring the Evil Eye: Reality and Remedy, An Islamic Perspective" by Dr. Ali Mohamed Salah, published by Loohpress in 2023, 1st edition.

BLACK MAGIC: HISTORICAL BACKGROUND AND THE INTERPLAY OF MEDICINE AND SPIRITUAL HEALING

Before delving further into this topic, I'd like to share insights from Dr. Ali Mushrif, a highly experienced scholar in contemporary times, particularly in the field of Ruqya (spiritual healing). With over two decades of experience in treating people, Dr. Mushrif highlights that a significant majority, approximately 99.9999%, of patients seeking treatment for ailments attributed to magic, evil eye, or jinn, were actually suffering from psychological or physiological issues. Despite their claims, their afflictions were not related to magic or supernatural phenomena. Dr. Mushrif emphasizes that these individuals were seeking help in the wrong place; their ailments required medical attention rather than spiritual intervention.[81]

This statement makes clear a critical reality: millions of Muslims who attribute their troubles to magic or other supernatural causes often overlook the importance of seeking medical evaluation. Rather than assuming a spiritual affliction, it's imperative for such individuals to undergo thorough medical examinations to accurately diagnose and address their conditions. This understanding highlights the necessity of approaching health issues with a holistic perspective, encompassing both spiritual and medical dimensions.

In the process of delivering this lecture, we aim to encapsulate various viewpoints and opinions to gain a comprehensive understanding of differing beliefs. It's important to note that presenting

---

81 The speech was delivered by Dr. Ali al-Mushrif at King Fahad Hospital in Al-Medina Al-Munawara in 1990, and I had the honor of being one of the attendees.

these perspectives does not signify our agreement with them. Rather, we present them to acknowledge the diversity of thought surrounding the topic. Before delving into specific divisions, let's first explore the historical origins of magic. As a prelude to this discussion, I began the lecture with a recitation of a lengthy verse.

In Chapter two, verse 102 of the Quran, Allah ﷻ mentions the time when magic was sent down during the reign of Solomon's kingdom. At that time, people followed magic, and Allah ﷻ explicitly states that those who practiced it were considered disbelievers. However, Solomon (peace be upon him) remained steadfast in his faith.

The Quranic verse also reveals that the magic was taught by two angels, Hārūt and Mārūt, in Babylon, Iraq. They warned against the temptation of magic, emphasizing that they were sent as a trial to the community, urging them not to stray from faith.

The teachings of these angels focused on causing discord between spouses, friends, siblings, and relatives. Despite their teachings, they could not harm anyone except by Allah's permission. Furthermore, they taught what harmed people without benefitting them. Allah ﷻ says: As stated in Sūra 2: Baqara,

"They followed what the evil ones gave out (falsely) against the power of Solomon; the blasphemers were not Solomon but the evil ones teaching men magic and such things as came down at Babylon to the angels Harut and Marut. But neither of these taught anyone (such things) without saying: "We are only for trial so do not blaspheme." They learned from them the means to sow discord between man and wife. But

they could not thus harm anyone except by God's permission. And they learned what harmed them not what profited them. And they knew that the buyers of (magic) would have no share in the happiness of the Hereafter. And vile was the price for which they did sell their souls if they but knew!."[82]

The Quran warns that those who indulge in such magic will not find success in the Hereafter. This verse contains ten significant points to be remembered.

---

82 Sūra 2: Baqara, Verse 102

SECTION TWO:
TYPES OF MAGIC: DEFINITIONS AND ISLAMIC RULINGS

MAGIC OF SEPARATION AND ILLEGAL PRACTICES: SYMPTOMS AND EFFECTS

The first type of magic mentioned by the scholars is the magic of separation, known as Siḥr al-Tafrīq. Religious scholars such as Ibn Kathīr have sought to define this form of magic. Siḥr al-Tafrīq is characterized by its aim to sow discord (fitna) between individuals. Its targets include friends, spouses, relatives, fathers and daughters, fathers and sons, mothers and daughters, and mothers and sons. The primary objective is to transform feelings of love into animosity. Individuals who were previously in harmonious relationships suddenly find themselves experiencing a shift in attitudes towards each other, transitioning from affection to enmity. This phenomenon aligns with what Allah ﷻ has elucidated in the Quranic verse I mentioned earlier: *"They separate one from another,"* indicating the deliberate intent to divide spouses.

Those who practice Siḥr al-Tafrīq do so with the specific aim of causing such divisions and ruptures in relationships. Ibn Kathīr, in his Tafsīr, elaborates on how Siḥr al-Tafrīq, the magic of separation, operates. He explains that one of the manifestations of this type of magic is that the husband may perceive his wife as unattractive or ill-mannered, or vice versa, leading to feelings of aversion between them. Similarly, the wife may view her husband in a negative light due to the influence of this magic. As a result, love between the couple turns into hatred.[83]

Symptoms of Siḥr al-Tafrīq include a sudden and unexplained shift in attitude towards one another. Despite there being no apparent reason for this change, individuals affected by this magic find themselves harboring feelings of animosity towards their partner.

Indeed, the symptoms illustrate the harmful and deceptive nature of Siḥr al-Tafrīq, or the magic of separation. This form of magic not only disrupts relationships but also undermines trust, fosters aversion, and distorts perceptions. It preys on vulnerabilities within relationships, turning minor issues into significant conflicts and driving a wedge between individuals who were once close. The insidiousness lies in its ability to manipulate emotions

---

83 Ibn Kathīr, https://shamela.ws/book/37048/336

and perceptions, leading to the deterioration of bonds that were once strong and loving.

Religious scholars explain that the process typically involves a person seeking the services of a sorcerer (sahir) to separate a specific individual from their spouse. The sorcerer requests the client to provide the names of both parties and their respective mothers. This information is then used in performing the magic ritual aimed at causing the desired separation.

LOVE, MAGIC, AND ILLEGAL PRACTICES: SYMPTOMS AND EFFECTS

The second type of magic is called Siḥr al-Tiwala, Siḥr al-Maḥaba which can be translated as the magic of love or infatuation. The Prophet Muḥammad ﷺ referenced this form of magic in a narration recorded by scholars such as Imam Aḥmad al-Ḥanbal, and Abū Dawūd al-Ḥākim. It's important to note that this type of magic does not involve lawful means such as recitation of Quranic verses, adherence to Sunnah practices, or supplications (adhkār). Siḥr al-Tiwala, along with the use of amulets and charms, is condemned by the Prophet Muḥammad ﷺ as acts of polytheism.

Zaynab the wife of 'Abdallah b. Mas'ud told that 'Abdallah saw a thread on her neck and asked what it was. When she told him that it was a thread over which a spell had been recited for her he took it, cut it up and said,

"You, family of 'Abdallah, are independent of

polytheism. I have heard God's messenger say that spells, charms and love-spells are polytheism." [84]

Ibn al-Athīr further elucidates this type of magic by explaining that it occurs when a person seeks to intensify love between themselves and their spouse to an extreme degree. While there's nothing inherently wrong with loving one's spouse, this specific manipulation of emotions through magic is deemed as an act of polytheism.

Performing this type of magic often involves acquiring personal belongings or bodily fluids from the targeted individual, such as a handkerchief or water. These items serve as conduits for the spellcasting process. The intention is for the affected person to interact with or be exposed to the enchanted item, leading them to be influenced by the magical effects. This process aims to manipulate the individual's emotions, thoughts, or behaviors according to the desires of the practitioner, resulting in the desired outcome, such as fostering love or causing discord. However, it's crucial to remember that such practices are condemned in Islam and are considered sinful and forbidden.

The condemnation of such practices stems from the belief that seeking supernatural assistance for matters of the heart infringes upon the belief in Allah's sole authority and power. Instead of relying on natural and lawful means to cultivate love and affection, resorting to magic is considered a form of shirk, or associating partners with Allah ﷻ.

Ibn al-Athīr's commentary delves deeper into the motives behind Siḥr al-Tiwala, the magic of love, and its implications. According to him, individuals resort to this form of magic with

---

84 Mishkat al-Masabih 4552 : Book 23, Hadith 39

the erroneous belief that they can manipulate Allah's will to fulfill their desires, particularly in matters of love and relationships. This presumption of exerting control over divine will constitutes a form of shirk, or polytheism, as it challenges the sovereignty of Allah ﷻ.[85]

The desire to win the affection of a spouse through magical means may stem from various motives, including greed and the intention to secure inheritance rights.

Additionally, some individuals may seek to intensify the effects of the magic, leading to a pervasive hatred towards all females, including close relatives.

This escalation poses a significant risk, as the intended target may eventually harbor animosity towards the one who initiated the magic, potentially leading to unintended consequences.

Ibn al-Athīr's insights highlight the grave spiritual dangers associated with engaging in acts of polytheism and attempting to manipulate divine will for personal gain. Such actions not only contravene Islamic principles but also carry the risk of severe repercussions, both spiritually and socially.

The process of Siḥr al-Tiwala, or the magic of love, typically involves the following steps:

- **Seeking the Services of a Sorcerer**: Either the husband or the wife may approach a sorcerer (sahir) with the desire to enhance the love and affection between them and their spouse.
- **Providing Personal Information**: The sorcerer

---

85 https://www.islamweb.net/ar/library/content/49/119

requests specific information, such as the names of the targeted individual and their mother. This information is crucial for the performance of the magic ritual.

- **Obtaining Personal Items:** The sorcerer may ask for personal items belonging to the targeted individual, such as clothing or accessories. These items are used in the magic ritual to establish a connection with the individual.

- **Performing the Magic Ritual:** The sorcerer performs the magic ritual, which typically involves blowing on or enchanting the personal items provided by the client. Incantations and symbols may also be used in the process.

- **Burying the Enchanted Item**: The sorcerer instructs the client to bury the enchanted item in a hidden place, either within the house or in a deserted area where it will not be easily discovered.

- **Concealing the Process**: The client is advised to keep the process secret and not reveal it to anyone, particularly the targeted individual. This secrecy is believed to enhance the effectiveness of the magic.

These steps outline how Sihr al-Tiwala is practiced, but it's important to note that engaging in such practices goes against Islamic teachings.

It's essential to adhere to lawful methods, such as seeking blessings through Quranic recitations (Ruqya) and adhering to the Sunnah, rather than resorting to forbidden practices like magic and amulets, which are considered acts of polytheism.

MAGIC OF FALSE APPEARANCE (SIḤR AL-KHAYĀL) AND ILLEGAL PRACTICES: SYMPTOMS AND EFFECTS

The third type of Siḥr is known as "false appearance," or Siḥr al-Khayāl. In this form of magic, static objects may appear to be in motion, while mobile objects may seem stationary. Similarly, small objects may appear large, and large objects may appear small. This distortion of perception can lead individuals to perceive reality inaccurately.

Allah ﷻ provides an example of this phenomenon in Sūra 20: Tā-Há, where He recounts how the followers of Pharaoh used their magic to create the illusion that their ropes and staffs were moving like snakes. This manipulation of perception instilled fear and awe in the heart of Moses.

Allah ﷻ says:

«They said : " O Moses ! Whether wilt thou That thou throw (first) Or that we be the first To throw ? "

He said, " Nay, throw ye First ! " Then behold Their ropes and their rods— So it seemed to him On account of their magic— Began to be in lively motion»[86]

Siḥr al-Khayal is often used for entertainment purposes, as seen in performances or on television shows where magicians create illusions to entertain audiences. However, it's important to remember that engaging in such practices is considered sinful in Islam and is prohibited. Muslims are advised to avoid involvement

---

86 Sūra 20: Tā-Há, 65-66

in magic and to seek lawful and ethical means of entertainment and amusement.

MAGIC OF LUNACY (AL-JUNUN) AND ILLEGAL PRACTICES: SYMPTOMS AND EFFECTS

The fourth type of magic is known as the magic of lunacy, or al-junoon. An incident recounted by Zahra Kharji ibn Zayed illustrates this phenomenon. Kharji's uncle embraced Islam, and on their journey back to the Prophet Muḥammad ﷺ, they encountered people who asked for their help in treating a man who was suffering from lunacy and was bound in chains. Upon their request, Kharji recited Surah Al-Fatiha, and miraculously, the afflicted man was cured.[87]

This narrative highlights the belief that magic can have tangible effects on individuals, causing physical and mental afflictions. It underscores the importance of seeking refuge in Allah ﷻ and relying on spiritual remedies, such as recitation of Quranic verses, in combating such afflictions.

Religious scholars explain that in cases of lunacy induced by magic, sorcerers harness the assistance of jinn, or demons, who enter the body of the afflicted individual and manipulate their brain cells, causing the symptoms of lunacy. While the veracity of such occurrences is known only to Allah ﷻ, Muslims do not deny the existence of Jinn or their potential influence on human beings.

Indeed, the Prophet Muḥammad ﷺ provided guidance on how to seek protection and healing from the effects of Siḥr.

---

87 Ṣaḥīḥ abu Daud, 3896, https://dorar.net/hadith/sharh/78464

One of the remedies he taught is to recite and regularly listen to the Holy Quran. The recitation of Quranic verses not only provides spiritual strength and protection but also brings peace and tranquility to the afflicted individual. By immersing oneself in the recitation of the Quran, one can find solace and relief from the distress caused by Siḥr. With faith in Allah's mercy and protection, seeking refuge in the Quran can serve as a powerful means of overcoming the harmful effects of magic, inshaAllah.

It's important to differentiate between ordinary dreams and nightmares and the effects of Siḥr, or magic. While dreams and nightmares are a natural part of the sleep cycle and often reflect one's thoughts, emotions, and experiences, Siḥr-induced dreams and nightmares involve the manipulation of one's subconscious by external forces.

Before attributing dreams or nightmares to Siḥr, it's essential to consider the individual's mental and emotional state before going to bed. Dreams are often influenced by one's thoughts, feelings, and experiences during the day. For example, if someone goes to bed hungry, they may dream of food. Similarly, emotions such as anger or romantic feelings can influence the content of dreams, leading to scenarios that reflect those emotions. These dreams are a normal part of the human experience and do not necessarily indicate the presence of Siḥr..

Furthermore, the feeling of being unable to run away or falling in dreams can often be attributed to physical sensations or positions during sleep rather than the effects of Siḥr. Adjusting one's physical position, such as stretching out a cramped leg, can sometimes alleviate these sensations.

While some may categorize certain dreams or nightmares as

Siḥr, it's crucial to approach such interpretations with caution and seek guidance from knowledgeable individuals or scholars. It's also important to maintain a strong connection with Allah ﷻ through regular prayers, recitation of Quranic verses, and seeking refuge in Him from any harmful influences, including Siḥr. With trust in Allah's protection and guidance, one can navigate through the challenges of dreams and nightmares with resilience and faith.

MAGIC OF ILLNESS

The concept of Siḥr of illness is one that requires careful consideration and discernment. While it's essential to seek medical attention for any physical ailments or discomforts, there may be instances where conventional medical treatments do not fully alleviate the symptoms.

If someone experiences persistent pain or illness despite medical examinations showing no apparent cause, it's reasonable to explore other possible explanations, including spiritual causes such as Siḥr. However, it's crucial to approach this with caution and seek guidance from knowledgeable individuals or scholars who are well-versed in Islamic teachings and spiritual remedies.

• CONTINUOUS BLEEDING OUTSIDE OF MENSES

The attribution of continuous bleeding outside of menses solely to Siḥr. While some may interpret ongoing bleeding as a sign of Siḥr, it's crucial to consider other potential factors that could contribute to this condition.

Medical research indicates that various factors, such as stress, depression, anxiety, hormonal imbalances, medication usage (such as morning-after pills), and certain medical conditions, can lead to irregular or prolonged bleeding outside of the menstrual cycle. These physiological and psychological factors can disrupt the normal menstrual pattern and cause confusion in menstrual bleeding. There is a prophetic tradition, where the Prophet Muḥammad ﷺ referred to continuous bleeding outside of menses as " This is a stroke of the Devil," On the authority of Hamnah daughter of Jahsh:

> **«Hamnah said my menstruation was great in quantity and severe. So I came to the Messenger of Allah (ﷺ) for a decision and told him. I found him in the house of my sister, Zaynab, daughter of Jahsh. I said: Messenger of Allah, I am a woman who menstruates in great quantity and it is severe, so what do you think about it? It has prevented me from praying and fasting. He said: I suggest that you should use cotton, for it absorbs the blood. She replied: It is too copious for that. He said: Then take a cloth. She replied: It is too copious for that, for my blood keeps flowing. The Messenger of Allah (ﷺ) said: I shall give you two commands; whichever of them you follow, that will be sufficient for you without the other, but you know best whether you are strong enough to follow both of them.He added: This is a stroke of the Devil...»[88]**

This narration provides spiritual insight into the matter. However, it's essential to approach such teachings with a balanced perspective, considering both spiritual and medical explanations for the phenomenon.

---

88 : Sunan Abi Dawud 287 : Book 1, Hadith 287

While acknowledging the possibility of spiritual influences, it's crucial not to overlook or dismiss the potential medical causes of irregular bleeding. Consulting with medical professionals and seeking appropriate healthcare interventions can help diagnose and address any underlying health issues contributing to abnormal bleeding patterns.

Individuals experiencing irregular bleeding should seek guidance from both medical and religious sources to ensure a comprehensive approach to their health and well-being. By considering all possible factors and seeking appropriate care, individuals can address their concerns effectively, inshaAllah.

MAGIC OF RELATIONSHIP HINDRANCES (MARRIAGE OR BUSINESS)

Additionally, some mention Siḥr of impeding marriage or business as a reason for their setbacks. They claim that Siḥr has hindered their marriage prospects or business success. However, attributing every failure or challenge in life to magic or evil eye overlooks other potential reasons, such as personal choices, external circumstances, or one's own shortcomings.

If we attribute every misfortune to magic or evil eye, we risk neglecting personal responsibility and failing to address underlying issues effectively. Failures could stem from various factors like ignorance, laziness, or lack of effort. Therefore, it's important not to hastily attribute difficulties solely to magic or supernatural causes.

MAGIC OF AL-UQM (STERILITY)

They also mention a form of Siḥr known as Siḥr of al-Uqm,

which causes sterility, preventing a woman from conceiving. However, as we've discussed based on the principles of 'aqīda, this assertion should be approached with caution. While acknowledging the possibility of spiritual influences, we must also consider medical factors that can contribute to infertility.

Infertility can result from various physiological, psychological, and medical reasons, including hormonal imbalances, reproductive disorders, genetic factors, lifestyle choices, and environmental factors. Therefore, attributing sterility solely to Siḥr overlooks the complexity of infertility and the need for comprehensive medical evaluation and treatment.

It's essential for individuals experiencing difficulties conceiving to seek guidance from both medical professionals and spiritual advisors, ensuring a holistic approach to addressing their concerns and exploring all possible factors contributing to infertility.

SECTION THREE:
EFFECTIVE STRATEGIES AGAINST MAGIC: GUIDANCE FROM ISLAMIC TEACHINGS

So, how can we effectively deal with Siḥr? Religious scholars have provided guidance on this matter, although the information may be scattered across various sources.

First and foremost, it's essential to understand that (***evil cannot be removed by evil***). This means that resorting to Siḥr to counteract the effects of Siḥr is not permissible. If someone has been afflicted by Siḥr, seeking help from a Shaykh or spiritual advisor who employs Siḥr to counter it would be incorrect and against Islamic principles.

PRACTICE OF RUQYA

The next crucial aspect in dealing with Siḥr is the practice of ruqya, which involves reciting specific verses from the Quran and supplications for healing and protection. The Prophet Muḥammad ﷺ emphasized the importance of ruqya and permitted its use as a means of treatment. He once informed his companions that there would be 70,000 people admitted to Paradise without any form of accountability. When asked about them, he explained that they were those who neither sought ruqya for themselves nor asked others to perform ruqya on their behalf. The narration is as follows: Ibn ʿAbbās (ﷺ) narrated that the Messenger of Allah ﷺ said,

"Seventy thousand people of my followers will enter Paradise without reckoning. They are those who do not practice ruqyah, do not take evil omens, and place their trust in their Rabb."[89]

This narration highlights the merit of self-administered ruqya for those afflicted by Siḥr. It implies that individuals can recite Quranic verses and supplications on themselves to seek healing from the effects of Siḥr. While the Prophet ﷺ did allow others to perform ruqya on him, it's noteworthy that he also engaged in the practice of ruqya for himself.

It's crucial to discern between legitimate and illegitimate forms of ruqya (spiritual healing) when seeking remedies for perceived afflictions like Siḥr. Legitimate ruqya, as prescribed by the Quran and Sunnah, involves reciting Quranic verses, supplications, and seeking Allah's protection and mercy. These methods are in

---

89 Ṣaḥīḥ al-Bukhārī, 6472

accordance with Islamic teachings and are considered effective in addressing spiritual ailments.

On the other hand, illegitimate ruqya involves practices that contradict Islamic principles, such as seeking assistance fromJinnor using obscure methods that lack clarity and understanding. Engaging in illegitimate ruqya can lead to further spiritual harm and is not permissible according to Islamic teachings.

It is noteworthy that if someone finds themselves suffering from the effects of Siḥr, they can engage in ruqya for themselves as a means of seeking relief and healing.

The minimum protection measures recommended are as follows:

Recite the last three Surahs of the Quran (Surah Al-Nas, Surah Al-Falaq, and Surah Al-Ikhlas).

Narrated 'Aisha: Whenever the Prophet ﷺ went to bed every night, he used to cup his hands together and blow over them after reciting Surat Al Ikhlas, Surat Al Falaq, and Surat An Nas, and then rub his hands over whatever parts of his body he was able to rub, starting with his head, face and front of his body. He used to do that three times. Bukhari 5017

Engage in the recitation of Surah Al-Baqarah.

Abū Hurayra reported Allah's Messenger ﷺ as saying: Do not make your houses as graveyards. Satan runs away from the house in which Surah Baqarah is recited. [90]

---

90 Muslim 780

Regularly remember and recite supplications as instructed by the Prophet in various situations, such as reciting adhkār (remembrances) when entering or exiting the house, using the toilet, traveling, and before and after consuming food and drink.[91]

However, individuals seeking spiritual healing should prioritize legitimate forms of ruqya guided by Quranic principles and the prophetic tradition. Consulting qualified religious scholars or practitioners who adhere to authentic Islamic teachings can help ensure that one receives proper guidance and support in addressing spiritual concerns. By reciting the Quran and supplications, individuals can harness the spiritual power of these verses to combat the harmful effects of Sihr, seeking Allah's protection and mercy in the process.

PHYSICAL AND EMOTIONAL RESPONSES DURING RUQYA

These physical and emotional responses during ruqya can indeed be indicators of the effectiveness of the treatment and the presence of Sihr. Crying, especially when specific Quranic verses addressing Sihr are recited, suggests a deep emotional reaction, potentially indicating that the individual is indeed affected by Sihr. Falling asleep during the recitation of the Quran can also be a sign, as it may signify a release of tension and a sense of peace overcoming the person.

Additionally, expressions like ironic looks, bulging eyes, or involuntary laughter can signify a disturbance in the affected in-dividual's emotional and mental state, potentially linked to the

---

91 Evil eye, Dr Ali, 122

effects of Sihr. Shivering or shaking may also manifest as physical reactions to the spiritual healing process.

However, it's important to approach these signs with caution and discernment. While they can provide valuable insights into the person's condition, they should be considered alongside other factors such as the person's overall behavior, history, and any corroborating evidence of Sihr.

It's important to maintain a balanced perspective when considering the phenomenon of Sihr and its potential impact on individuals. While acknowledging the existence of Sihr as described in prophetic tradition, it's also crucial to approach any perceived symptoms or experiences with a rational and discerning mindset.

As you've rightly noted, not every unusual sensation or reaction necessarily indicates the presence of Sihr. Understanding the specific types of Sihr described in the prophetic tradition can help differentiate genuine cases from other explanations. This can prevent unnecessary anxiety or undue attribution of ordinary experiences to supernatural causes.

REMEMBERING ALLAH ﷻ AND RECITING SUPPLICATIONS

Remembering Allah ﷻ and reciting supplications are powerful means of seeking protection and healing from afflictions such as Sihr. The Prophet Muhammad ﷺ taught specific prayers and invocations to recite for seeking refuge from harm. For example, reciting certain phrases, such as "Bismillah" seven times, along with supplications seeking protection from evil, can be highly effective. Instead of solely relying on others to perform ruqya or seeking magical solutions, believers are encouraged to turn to these prescribed prayers and remembrances of Allah ﷻ.

The simplicity and accessibility of these remedies underscore the importance of utilizing them regularly. Additionally, it's essential to recite these prayers in Arabic, the language of the Quran, with sincerity and understanding, as this enhances their effectiveness. Ultimately, placing trust in Allah's words, His names, and attributes, and diligently reciting the prescribed supplications can provide spiritual healing and protection against malevolent forces.

ENGAGING IN NIGHT PRAYER

Engaging in night prayer, particularly during the serene hours when the world is quiet and dark, offers a profound opportunity for spiritual connection and supplication. Prostrating before Allah ﷻ with devotion and sincerity during this time holds immense significance. The Prophet Muḥammad ﷺ emphasized the closeness to Allah ﷻ experienced during prostration, highlighting its importance in our worship. Abū Hurayra reported: The Messenger of Allah, ﷺ said,

"The servant is closest to his Lord during prostration, so increase your supplications therein."[92]

By dedicating a substantial portion of time to night prayer, focusing on lengthy recitations and prolonged prostration, believers can strengthen their bond with the Divine and seek protection from adversities, including the effects of magic.

---

92 Ṣaḥīḥ Muslim 482

ATTENDING CONGREGATIONAL PRAYERS

Attending congregational prayers is also considered a beneficial treatment, as stated by the Prophet Muḥammad ﷺ. When the call to prayer (Ādhān) is recited, Satan flees to avoid hearing it. However, he returns to distract worshippers during the prayer itself, leading to absent-mindedness and a lack of focus.

Abū Hurayra reported the Messenger of Allah ﷺ as saying:

«When Satan hears the call to prayer, he turns back and breaks the wind so as not to hear the call being made, but when the call is finished he turns round and distracts (the minds of those who pray), and when he hears the Iqama, he again runs away so as not to hear its voice and when it subsides, he comes back and distracts (the minds of those who stand for prayer».[93]

Therefore, individuals can seek protection from Satan's influence and strengthen their connection with Allah ﷺ By participating in congregational prayers. This communal act of worship helps believers remain vigilant against distractions and maintain their focus on the prayers, thereby mitigating the effects of evil eye and other spiritual afflictions.

1- GATHERING IN PLACES WHERE ALLAH ﷺ IS REMEMBERED

Gathering in places where Allah is remembered, such as mosques or gatherings of believers, carries immense spiritual significance. The Prophet Muḥammad ﷺ emphasized the blessings and mercy that descend upon such gatherings, with

---

93 Sahih Muslim 389a : Book 4, Hadith 19

angels surrounding those present. One can experience spiritual upliftment and protection from malevolent forces by actively participating in these gatherings and immersing oneself in the remembrance of Allah ﷻ.

2- CUPPING THERAPY (AL-ḤIJĀMA)

Cupping Therapy, known as al-Ḥijāma, is recommended as a treatment method to remove stagnant and toxic blood from specific areas of the body. This procedure can potentially aid in alleviating symptoms associated with Siḥr. The Prophet Muḥammad ﷺ endorsed cupping as a beneficial practice, affirming its effectiveness in promoting health and well-being. Jābir b. ʿAbdallah (ﷺ) also narrated that, **"I heard the Prophet ﷺ saying, "If there is any good in your medicines, then it is in a gulp of honey, a cupping [Ḥijāma] operation, or branding (cauterization), but I do not like to be (cauterized) branded."**[94]

-   THE BEST TIME TO GET CUPPED

Narrated by Abū Hurayra (ﷺ); **"The Prophet ﷺ said: If anyone has himself cupped on the 17th, 19th and 21st it will be a remedy for every disease."**[95]

The 17th, 19th and 21st [of the month] mentioned here is referring to the Lunar calendar. It is generally understood that when the Moon is full, it has the strongest possible gravitational pull on the earth and its inhabitants.

The effect in human beings is that the volatile bodily fluids and

---

94 Sahih Al Bukhari Volume 7, Book 71, Number 603.

95 Sunan Abi Dawood Book 28, Hadith 3852. Classed as Hasan by Sh. Al Albaani (rahimahullah).

humors are pulled into the uppermost part of the body during the 1 day either side of the full moon (and on the full moon). As the phases of the full Moon subside to the 17th, 19th and 21st of the lunar month, the volatile humours subside too and the underlying humours are pulled up into their place. It is within these underlying bodily fluids and humours that the patient might be suffering toxicity. Once these underlying humours come close to the skins surface within the upper body, any toxicity or excess can easily be extracted through Ḥijāma.[96] Therefore, incorporating Ḥijāma alongside other permissible remedies may contribute to the overall treatment of Siḥr, in shā Allah.

3- CONSUMING SEVEN ʿAJWA DATES

Consuming seven ʿAjwa dates early in the morning, as mentioned in a hadith recorded by Imam al-Bukhāri, is recommended as a means of protection against harm and magic. The Prophet Muḥammad ﷺ assured that those who eat these dates with sincere belief will be safeguarded from the effects of harm and magic.

Narrated Saʿd: Allah's Messenger ﷺ said, **"He who eats seven ʿAjwa dates every morning, will not be affected by poison or magic on the day he eats them."**[97]

It's essential to have complete faith in the prophetic guidance and the efficacy of ʿAjwaʿAjwa dates as a protective measure.

---

96 https://www.harrowcuppingclinic.co.uk/narrations

97 Ṣaḥīḥ al-Bukhārī 5445, And Sahih Muslim 204 , https://sunnah.com/bukhari:5445

4- DRINKING ZAMZAM WATER

Jabir Bin abdullahi said :"I heard the Messenger of Allah (ﷺ) say:

" The water of Zamzam is for whatever it is drunk for". [98]

5- DRINKING HONEY

Allah ﷻ says:

"Then eat from all the fruits and follow the ways of your Lord laid down [for you]." There emerges from their bellies a drink, varying in colors, in which there is healing for people. Indeed in that is a sign for a people who give thought". [99]

Ibn Kathīr commented on this verse by saying:

"(in which there is a cure for men.) meaning there is a cure in honey for diseases that people suffer from. Some of those who spoke about the study of Prophetic medicine said that if Allah had said, 'in which there is the cure for men,' then it would be the remedy for all diseases, but He said, 'in which there is a cure for men,' meaning that it is the right treatment for every "cold" disease, because it is "hot," and a disease should be treated with its opposite". [100]

The prophetic tradition: Abu Sa'id Khudri reported:

"that a person came to Allah's Apostle (ﷺ) and told

---

98 Sunan Ibn Majah 3062

99 Al-Nahl verse: 69

100 Ibn Kathīr: Tafsīr Surat Al-Nahl, Quran .com

him that his brother's bowels were loose. Thereupon, Allah's Messenger (ﷺ) said: Give him honey. So he gave him that and then came and said: I gave him honey, but it has only made his bowels more loose. He said this three times, and then he came the fourth time, and he (the Holy Prophet) said: Give him honey. He said: I did give him, but it has only made his bowels more loose, whereupon Allah's Messenger (ﷺ) said: Allah has spoken the truth, and your brother's bowels are in the wrong. So he made him drink (honey), and he was recovered". [101]

6- TREATING IT WITH BLACK SEEDS

Abū Hurayra narrated that the Messenger of Allah ﷺ him said:

"Use this black seed. For indeed, it contains a cure for every disease except As-Sam," And As-Sam is death." [102]

7- DEALING WITH MAGICIANS AND ENCHANTED OBJECTS

Another crucial step in dealing with Siḥr is to uncover and neutralize the items used by the magician or sorcerer. This might involve searching for hidden objects or materials that have been enchanted or manipulated for Siḥr purposes. For instance, it could be a thread buried in the ground, a handkerchief that mysteriously reappears in the house, or any other suspicious item.

Once these items are identified, it's essential to remove and

---

101 Sahih Muslim 2217

102 Jami` at-Tirmidhi 2041

destroy them promptly. This could involve burning them, discarding them far away from the house, or any other method that ensures they are rendered ineffective. By eliminating these enchanted objects, one can nullify the effects of Sihr and thwart the intentions of the sorcerer. This act serves to protect the affected individual and their household from further harm, insha'Allah subhanahu wa ta'ala.

If the magician responsible for the Sihr is identified, there is a recommendation to compel them to undo their harmful magic. However, Imam An-Nawi highlights the practical challenges in directly confronting the magician. Typically, they will deny involvement and may even react aggressively.

In cases where the magician's identity is established through official channels, such as government authorities or other credible sources, there is a duty to hold them accountable and force them to reverse the effects of their Sihr. This approach, sanctioned by scholars, provides a legal and effective means to address the situation, insha'Allah.

Finally, maintaining trust in Allah's protection and seeking appropriate remedies, such as engaging in acts of worship, seeking medical advice when needed, and reciting Quranic verses for spiritual healing, can provide comfort and empowerment in addressing any challenges one may face.

BIBLIOGRAPHY

BOOKS:

Al-Quran al-Kreem

Abd al-Karim 'Ubaydat: 'Alam al-Jinn fi Daw' al-Kitab wa'l-Sunnah, p. 447;

'Ali al-'Ubaydi: al-Mawsu'ah al-Shamilah li Madhhab al-Ruhiyyah al-Hadithah wa Tahdir al-Arwah, 2/604.

Al-Bukhari, Imam. 1996. Ṣaḥīḥ al-Bukhārī. Riyad: Maktaba Dar-us-Salam.

An-Nasa'i, Abu Abdur Rahman. n.d. Sunan An-Nasa'i. Dar Al Maarifah.

As-Sijistan, Abu Dawud Sulayman ibn al-Ash'ath. n.d. Sunan Abi Dawud. Riyad: Dar Al Maarifah.

al-Ṭabarī, Abu Ja'far Muḥammad ibn Jarir. n.d. Tafsīr IBN JARIR al-Ṭabarī - JAMI' AL-BAYAN 'AN TA WIL AL-QURAN. Dar Kotob Al-Ilmiyah

At-Tirmidhi, Muḥammad ibn 'Issa. 1978. SUNAN AT-TIRMIDHI. Beirut: Darul Fikr Dīn Ahmed, 1997.

Exploring the Evil Eye: Reality and Remedy, An Islamic Perspective" by Dr. Ali Mohamed Salah, published by Loohpress in 2023, 1st edition

WEBSITE:

Ephesians 4:27 https://www.bibleref.com/Ephesians/4/Ephesians-4-27.html

Ephesians 6:11 https://www.cgg.org/index.cfm/library/verses/id/5334/satan-as-tempter-verses.htm

Farhana Akter, Mar 30, 2024 https://fakter-64263.medium.com/your-companions-7e888d027c6e

Fatwa https://www.islamweb.net/en/fatwa/239806/meaning-of-the-hadeeth-satan-urinated-in-his-ear

Genesis 3:13 https://www.cgg.org/index.cfm/library/verses/id/5334/satan-as-tempter-verses.htm

Genesis 3:1-5 https://www.cgg.org/index.cfm/library/verses/id/5334/satan-as-tempter-verses.htm

Tafsīr surah Jinn, ayah 6 https://myislam.org/surah-jinn/ayat-6/

Tafsīr al-Dabari, https://shamela.ws/book/7798/14612

The Holy Quran, Translation by A. Yusuf Ali https://quranyusufali.com/49/

Ibn 'Abd al-Barr, al-Istizkar, 8/363 https://waqfeya.net/book.php?bid=1457

Ibn Kathīr, https://shamela.ws/book/37048/336

Isaiah 14:12 https://www.cgg.org/index.cfm/library/verses/id/5334/satan-as-tempter-verses.htm

James 1:14-15, https://www.biblegateway.com/passage/?search=James%201%3A14-15&version=NIV

John 8:44 https://www.cgg.org/index.cfm/library/verses/id/5334/satan-as-tempter-verses.htm

Luke 4:13 https://www.cgg.org/index.cfm/library/verses/id/5334/satan-as-tempter-verses.htm

Majmuʿ al-Fatawa, 11/307-309, https://dorar.net/en/aqadia/

Matthew 6:13 https://www.cgg.org/index.cfm/library/verses/id/5334/satan-as-tempter-verses.htm

Mishkat al-Masabih,https://sunnah.com/mishkat

Narrations from ahadeeth regarding Ḥijāma https://www.harrowcuppingclinic.co.uk/narrations

Peter 5:8, https://goodnewsuk.com/bible-helps/1-peter-58-10

Peter 5:8, https://www.biblegateway.com/passage/?-search=1%20Peter%205%3A8&version=NIV

Question and answer, https://www.islamweb.net/ar/library/content/49/119

Ṣaḥīḥ abu Daud, 3896, https://dorar.net/hadith/sharh/78464

Ṣaḥīḥ al-Bukhārī Volume 2, Book 22, Hadith Number 301. https://hadithcollection.com/sahihbukhari/sahih-bukhari-book-22-actions-while-praying/sahih-bukhari-volume-002-book-022-hadith-number-301

Sakat, Ahamad Asmadi, et al. "The jinn, devil and Satan: A review on Qur'anic concept." *Mediterranean Journal of Social Sciences* 6.5 (2015): 540-546. https://www.researchgate.net/publication/282424716_The_Jinn_Devil_and_Satan_AReview_on_Qur'anic_Concept

Sunan Abi Dawood Book 28, Hadith 3852. https://sunnah.com/abudawud

Sunan Ibn Majah 1330 : Book 5, Hadith https://sunnah.com/ibnmajah

Tafsīr al-Rāzī, https://tafsir.app/alrazi/51/55

INDEX

Symbols

'Abdallah b. Mas'ūd 6, 7
'Abdallah b. 'Umar 8
'Ajwa 101
'Aqīda 50
'Ifrīt 3, 4, 6
'Umar 44

A

ablution 26, 28, 31, 32, 62
Abrahamic faiths 14
Abū al-Sā'ib 48
Abū Dardā' 33
Abū Dawūd al-Ḥākim 81
Abū Hurayra 28, 32, 45, 46, 50, 65,
        95, 98, 99, 100, 103
Abū Sa'īd al-Khudrī 48
Adam 8, 9, 10, 16, 21, 22, 32
Ādhān 44, 65, 99
adhkār 54, 81, 96
Ahl al-Ḍalāl 41
Ahl al-Sunnah 41
Aḥmad al-Ḥanbal 81
Aḥmad Khan 10
al-Ghazzālī 52
al-Ḥijāma 100
al-Jānn 4
al-Jinn 4, 5, 59, 105
Allāh vii
al-Muwaṭṭa' 43
al-Nasafī 11
al-Qurṭubī 27, 31

al-Rāzī 12, 108
al-Shāfi'ī 52
al-Shawkānī 8
al-Ṭabarī 5, 12, 105
al-Ṭāghūt 6
amulets 81, 84

B

Babylon xv, 76
Badr 42, 43, 44
Bible 13, 14, 15, 16, 18, 19
biblical 15
black cat 44, 45
black dogs 44
BLACK SEEDS 103
blazing fire 20
Book of Job 16

C

Canidae family 38
charms 81, 82
Christianity xvi, 8, 14, 63
creed 50
Cupping Therapy 100

D

Daḥḥāk 11
dates 21, 101
Devil 3, 6, 8, 10, 12, 89, 107
Dhikr 27, 31